Jean-Paul Thommen / Ansgar Richter (Eds.)

Management Consulting Today

Jean-Paul Thommen / Ansgar Richter (Eds.)

Management Consulting Today

Strategies for a Challenging Environment

GABLER

Bibliographic information published by Die Deutsche Bibliothek
Die Deutsche Bibliothek lists this publication in the Deutsche Nationalbibliografie;
detailed bibliographic data is available in the Internet at <http://dnb.ddb.de>.

Prof. Dr. Jean-Paul Thommen is Professor of Business Administration, in particular Organisational Behaviour and Human Resource Management, at the European Business School in Oestrich-Winkel, Germany. He is also Adjunct Professor at the University of Zurich and a Visiting Lecturer at the University of St Gallen.

Ansgar Richter, PhD, is Assistant Professor of Organisation and Human Resource Management at the European Business School in Oestrich-Winkel, Germany.

1st edition November 2004

All rights reserved
© Betriebswirtschaftlicher Verlag Dr. Th. Gabler/GWV Fachverlage GmbH, Wiesbaden 2004

Gabler is a company of Springer Science+Business Media.
www.gabler.de

Registered and/or industrial names, trade names, trade descriptions etc. cited in this publication are part of the law for trade-mark protection and may not be used free in any form or by any means even if this is not specifically marked.

Cover design: Ulrike Weigel, www.CorporateDesignGroup.de
Printing and binding: Wilhelm & Adam, Heusenstamm
Printed on acid-free paper
Printed in Germany

ISBN 3-409-12584-1

Editorial Preface

Jean-Paul Thommen and Ansgar Richter

Over the past 20 years, the consulting sector has undergone massive changes. Between 1995 and 2000 alone, the size of the global consulting market, measured by total revenues, more than doubled, growing from $51 billion in 1995 to more than $110 billion in 2000. Although the growth of the industry stalled between 2001 and 2003, it has since begun to rebound again. With the rise of the industry, its importance from an economic point of view has increased, too. According to the European Federation of Management Consulting Associations, management consulting revenues have risen as a percentage of European GDP from 0.12% in 1994 to 0.48% in 2002. In the context of this development, the importance of consulting firms as employers has increased, and many graduates from business schools and from other disciplines consider careers in consulting. At the same time, the nature of consulting firms, and of the services they provide, has changed significantly, with new players entering the market and clients demanding different types of services.

The purpose of this book is to provide the perspectives of leading consultants and industry observers in Europe on these developments, and on the trends going forward. Our intention in collecting contributions from senior consulting professionals was to gather views on the dramatic changes in the consulting sector from *within* that industry. Therefore, we sought to collate the perspectives of authors who can share rich, first-hand experience and in-depth insight, and who hold positions of responsibility within their firms. The contributions are therefore intentionally shaped by the experiences of the contributors in their respective firms, and by their personal views on where their professional practice is going. In many places, the texts are enriched with examples from the strategies, structures, management methods and cultures of the organisations represented by the authors.

Management Consulting Today comprises three interrelated yet distinct sections. The chapters in the first section are all concerned with the changing nature of consulting as an activity. The contributions in the second section look at how consulting firms are evolving, and the implications of the trends that we are seeing in the consulting market for the management of consulting organisations. The final section investigates the development of the consulting industry as a whole. Therefore, the book begins by analysing the most elementary unit of the consulting phenomenon – consulting as an activity – and then broadens the perspective to look at how the changing nature of consulting affects the firms providing these services, and the sector as a whole.

All texts in the book are original contributions. The idea to publish *Managing Consulting Today* emerged after we had invited some of the authors to give presentations at the European Business School, our home institution, in Winter 2003. Following a series of fascinating lectures, many of the participants asked us to make the texts available to the wider public. In order to provide rich and encompassing perspectives on the development of the consulting sector, we invited further contributors to join the team, and many of them agreed to do so. We are deeply grateful to all who have taken the time and the energy to contribute to this book. In particular, we would like to thank David Maister, the author of the classic *Managing the Professional Service Firm* (1993) and of many other groundbreaking books on consulting and consulting firms, for agreeing to write a thought-provoking foreword to this book.

We owe much to the people who helped to shape this book. First, we are indebted to the publisher, Gabler Verlag, in particular to Ulrike Lörcher and Katharina Harsdorf, for their professional support of the publication project. Second, we acknowledge the work of Marco Trautmann, Caroline Merk, and in particular of Linda Albrecht, who have helped us greatly to prepare the manuscript for publication. Without their assistance, the work on this book could not have been completed. Finally, we would like to thank our colleagues at the European Business School, and in particular its leadership. The European Business School provides an unrivalled atmosphere for studying the development of the consulting sector, and we are grateful for being able to work in this environment. Our thanks go to all those who have supported us in publishing this book.

Wiesbaden, October 2004   Jean-Paul Thommen
                                                                    Ansgar Richter

Foreword

David H. Maister

This stimulating book covers a wide range of issues. The diversity of subjects reveals the uncertain state of the consulting profession: There are a large number of viable options on positioning, ways of working with clients, ownership, firm culture, knowledge management, and much more. These articles are very persuasive, and provide a multitude of suggestions on what firms must do well to compete. While there are some differences of view, there are many areas of consensus.

Books serve the reader in two ways: The first is providing conclusions, insights and points of view ("what must be done"). This book is rich in such lessons. The second is stimulating the reader to think about the implications of those conclusions ("how will these things be achieved"). Here are some of the "how" questions this excellent book stimulates:

Where do we get new skills?

Many of the authors stress the continued evolution of consulting to include skills in creating and building relationships, earning trust, working with (not just for) the client and serving the client by creating experiences, not just transferring knowledge.

What is interesting about this (undoubtedly correct) perspective is that few consultants are formally trained in these skills, certainly not in their formal university training, and perhaps not by their firms. Indeed the state of the art in understanding these emotional, interpersonal skills is far behind our ability to transfer technical, analytical skills and knowledge. A number of authors in this book report the importance of knowledge transfer in consulting firms. Yet how many firms have figured out a way to develop and share the softer client interaction skills that so many people say are critical in consulting?

No doubt some firms have made real progress in this area, but their methods are not in the public domain. For the rest, the questions remain: How do we speed up the acquisition of client contact skills, not just for selling, but to transform the consulting experience for the client? Does the (increasing) need for these skills change the way we think about recruiting and staffing of the consulting firm?

Do we really know how organisations work?

A related question prompted by the chapters of this book is: Do consultants really have the skills to bring about major change in their client organisations? As

Mintzberg has pointed out in his recent book (Mintzberg, 2004), there is big difference between knowing a lot about business and knowing how to manage, and most of us consultants are trained in the former, not the latter. You can be very good at the analytical skills of figuring out what a client should do, and also be completely unprepared in mobilising the client organisation to achieve it. As with the client relations topic, the crucial distinction here is between intellectual skills (which consultants have in abundance) and the emotional, interpersonal, psychological and social skills needed to bring about change in large organisations.

A number of consulting firms have "Change Management" practices (referred to in this book) but the challenge is greater than that. If we, as consultants, are to achieve real results (as so many of this book's authors say we must) then all of us, not just the change management specialists, must learn about management and how it works. We must all learn about such subjects as energising people, obtaining buy-in, building mission-oriented teams. If we do not, then we will achieve less for our clients. We will have been "right" but not "helpful". There is a lot of intellectual satisfaction in being right, but not a profitable career!

Do we know how to manage people? Do we do it?

A third area of reflection prompted by this book is the role of people management inside the consulting firm. While a number of authors make reference to the importance of the topic, it is not explored in any great depth, certainly not in comparison to the time spent on client topics.

This is not in any way a criticism of the authors represented here. Instead, it is an accurate reflection of the relative proportion of time spent on these topics by consultants (and other professional firms). As with many of this book's topics, we have a good sense of what we want to achieve, but do not always have a clear understanding of how to bring it about. Do we really know how to attract and select those most likely to succeed as consultants? Do we really know how to create cross-boundary collaboration in a multidimensional consulting firm? Do we really know how to achieve fast skill-building in junior staff (not just knowledge transfer). Do we know how to get people to do things for the good of the firm, and not act independently?

As before, some firms will answer "yes", but the approaches and methodologies of effective people management in consulting firms remain proprietary. There is far less debate about how to mobilise a firm of consultants than there is on how to influence clients. Yet a good case can be made that effectiveness in managing internally is a logical prerequisite for achieving great things externally. Clients receive only what the consultants deliver. So, a superior ability to excite and energise one's consultants, get them to collaborate, share and develop new skills would clearly result in a competitive advantage on the client marketplace.

Do we manage?

A final topic surfaced in this book is the issue of managing and leading within the firm. It is noted that, in most firms, those who occupy managerial positions rarely spend all their time on the managerial, leading or coaching function. Rather, to a greater or lesser extent, they also serve clients and run engagements.

Experience varies, but the result of this dual role in many firms is that, whenever it comes to a choice, the client service role takes precedence over the managerial role. If managing means active efforts to raise the performance of team members through guidance, exhortation, cajoling, inspiring, following–up, nagging and helping, then little managing takes place in many consulting firms. Firms do administration well, and most have good performance metrics to monitor and reward performance. However, they spend little time on managing individuals and small teams to improve the performance. In most firms, as we have seen, this is because an external client activity will always dominate an internal managerial activity.

Wisely, a number of the authors of this book point to the role of culture and values in making the consulting firm work. They are correct to stress the power of cultures and values, and also to suggest that not all consulting firms have these topics working effectively for them. The question arises, what does it really take to create and sustain a strong, productive culture? What do you have to do to ensure that your firm has, and adheres to, a common set of values?

One of the things you must do is manage. A value is not a value if it is not enforced. That requires a manager to know what is going on and, whenever there is a departure from the value, have the time and inclination to intervene (in real time). If a departure from living the value receives no reaction or consequences, it will not be a value for long.

A good case could be made that this will have to change, and that consulting firms will have to give more attention to management. Consider some of the changes explored by the authors of this book: new services, multidisciplinary structures, globalisation, outsourcing, knowledge-sharing. All these trends suggest that we are creating more complex organisations, not less. And that will, I believe, cause firms to re-examine what kind of management approaches they will need to accommodate the changes. The authors of this book have served us well in pointing out what needs to be done. We all have a lot to do to make it a reality.

References

Mintzberg, Henry (2004): Managers not MBAs, Berret-Koehler Publishers, San Francisco.

Contents

PART I

THE CHANGING NATURE OF CONSULTING

The Truth Seekers

Dieter Heuskel

1. Strategies, not stories

> *"We believe that every business worthy of survival can be even more*
> *profitable, more productive, more satisfying and rewarding to its*
> *employees and more responsive to its customers while selling at ever*
> *lower real prices. '*

Bruce D. Henderson, BCG Founder

A company, if it is publicly listed, must convince investors and shareholders that the capital deployed today will be the added value of tomorrow. It is not the present that counts, but the future. This is why both shareholders and stakeholders need "stories": stories that tell – plausibly – how and why the company will assert itself successfully in the markets of the future. The more uncertainty, the more unknown variables there are in the story – the use of new technologies, expansion into new markets, or the development of new business models – the greater the difference between Today and Tomorrow, and greater scope for expectations.

Beyond the extremes demonstrated by the New Economy boom, it is true: attractiveness is an exciting story, and this attractiveness is reflected by the stock price, the sum of present earnings and expectations for the future. This is one side. The other side is that a company achieves long-term success, that is, growth under changing competitive circumstances, not with its "story," but with its – realized – strategy.

Bruce Henderson, a pioneer of strategy consulting and the founder of The Boston Consulting Group (1998, first published in 1973), defined strategy as the "perpetual search for sustainable competitive advantage and its implementation in the organisation." Consultants encourage, guide and accelerate this process. This applies to both dimensions: strategic reorientation and organisational optimisation.

The management consulting profession emerged and established itself at a time when the demands made of the management of large companies had increased dramatically. In the 1950s and 1960s, the competition in many industries intensified, among other reasons due to stronger international trade relations. For example, many companies in the United States were challenged by the upswing in European exports – and later by the flourishing Japanese automobile industry – with regard to price, quality, and customer orientation.

While the consulting work during these years was characterized primarily by questions of organisational optimisation, productivity improvement and cost reduction, the focus of strategy consulting changed repeatedly with the competitive developments of subsequent decades, turning to growth concepts in the 1970s, for instance, followed by reorganisation in the 1980s, and e-commerce and new value chain architectures in the 1990s.

Strategy consulting is based on the necessity to continually set oneself apart from the competition. The longer a market situation persists, the more similar the "responses" of the market players will be, and the lower the gains from differentiation. The "fade phenomenon," as it is called, applies to all industries and markets. Only those who manage to break out of the dynamics of convergence are able to escape the negative spiral of sinking margins that results from a low level of differentiation among competitors.

The content has changed, but the basic aim of consulting has stayed the same: to help companies escape the fade trap with outside, cross-operation and industry know-how. The methods and instruments of analysis have changed, but the basics are the same: the special relationship between consultants and their clients that makes effective consulting possible.

Strategy consulting is always a collaborative search for the best of numerous options for action. Successful strategies are case-specific solutions, not general answers. Concepts are important, while "recipes" are seldom much help.

The results of strategy consulting are due to a non-standardized process, jointly driven—and never exactly calculable—by consultants and their clients.

Strategy development is therefore always the result of a unique, unconventional search for the best solution for the specific case at hand. BCG understands this process as a virtuous circle consisting of three factors: Insight, impact, and trust.

2.   Insight – Diversity yields wisdom

"Our future lies in forever being able to be at the cutting edge, well in advance of the general state-of-the-art. When we are no longer able to do this, we will relinquish our role to others and wish them well."

Bruce D. Henderson

Seeing new things is the precondition for creating new things.

Successful growth strategies call for an accurate assessment of the market's developments and the company's own situation and position. Which trends characterize the industry? Where does the company stand in the marketplace? What resources are available? And above all: Where do we want to go? Without a map, without a destination, or without a fitness check, every departure would turn into an incalculable adventure.

Fade: The Fate of all Business Ventures ?

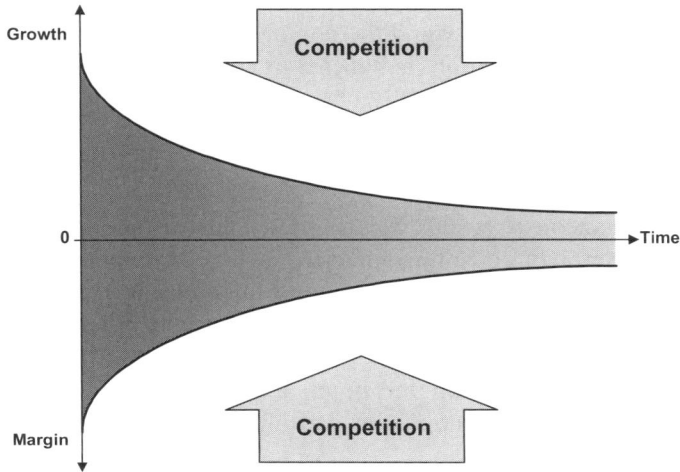

Fig. 1. Fade: The fate of all business ventures?

Our Aspiration

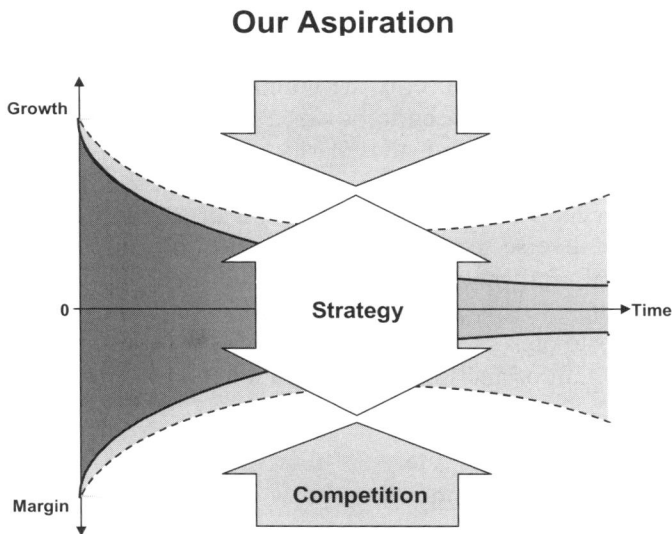

Fig. 2. Our aspiration

Consultants can play a crucial, trend-setting role in the analysis phase of strategy development. There are two reasons for this. First, the (consultant's) view from outside complements and expands the internal perspective. Secondly, the reason for an analysis of the industry and the company or classical benchmarking used to determine the current position, is not just to collect, edit and interpret the data; the prime objective is to additionally challenge familiar convictions and to discover blind spots. This presupposes that consultants have a good understanding of the company and the industry it operates in, and are capable of providing inspiration from "outside the industry."

The ability to simultaneously render insider knowledge of the industry and the external perspective useful in consulting practice is less a personal skill than a systemic one. Almost all the major management consultancies have the elaborated structures of a knowledge organisation that combines in practice the expertise and experience of experts for various industries, corporate functions, products and regions. At BCG, it is what we call the practice groups that pool, refine and communicate the expertise of the individual consultants in the form of a matrix (industries/functions).

The significance attached to the dimension known as "insight" for the entire consulting process is reflected in consulting practice. Each project commences with the often difficult decision on the ideal composition of the project team according to experience and expertise, external inspiration and internal know-how. Depending on past experience and objectives, the initial positions of the consultants on the one hand and the people responsible in the client company on the other hand may, in practice, be very far apart – a diversity of perceptions and interpretations, an ideal condition for development.

A period of intensive initiation into the situation of the client company at all levels forms the basis and the backbone of the consulting process. How questions are formulated, how problems and targets are defined determines the course of the project and its results. Furthermore, there is a second "balancing act" that consultants have to master. This concerns the complexity of varying individual and market-specific conditions that need to be taken into account when analysing and selecting strategic options, and the clarity – and "simplicity" – that characterizes an effective, logical strategy.

Patterns become evident in the internal exchange of knowledge gained by individual consultants in diverse settings. These form the "raw materials" used to develop company-neutral, and mostly industry-neutral, concepts, which in turn can be used as instruments of analysis and regulatory frameworks in the consulting work. Four examples – from four decades of BCG consulting activity – illustrate the interconnection of analysis and application, and theory and practice, in strategy development.

2.1 The Experience Curve (1966)

Strategy development is the deliberate reinforcement of – positive – differences in the marketplace. One of the key considerations is the company's cost situation.

The "experience curve" – related to but deliberately kept separate from the learning curve – was discovered by BCG in its consulting work, and was introduced as a generally valid rule applicable across all industries and cost items for the first time in 1966. It describes the cost development of a product as a rule of thumb: "The cost of value creation falls by around 20 to 30 percent with every doubling of cumulative experience." In this context, the term itself does not mean that "experience" alone in the narrow sense is responsible for the steady fall in costs; rather, "experience" stands for the interplay of economies of scale, the learning curve and returns on investment, substitution effects and specialization. Hardly any company will achieve economies of scale without boosting its volumes or will boost its volumes without gaining experience.

This insight gives rise to pragmatic implications of tremendous significance for competitive positioning and boosting market share. Thus, costs fall faster as growth accelerates. The differing growth rates in turn determine how quickly the profit margins of the competition shift. Demonstrated in numerous case studies, the general validity of the experience curve in various cost elements like advertising, overheads, marketing, development costs or manufacturing, can be used as an indicator: blips in the expected cost curves indicate symptoms that need to be investigated. At the same time, the experience curve makes it possible to reliably predict that one competitor can, and should, have lower costs than another, thus facilitating a forecast on the development of market share, if a competitor with lower costs succeeds in supplying the same products at the same margins to the same customers with similar expectations.

The experience curve formulated a contradiction to underlying assumptions of classical business theory, which works on the basis of a finite minimum cost as a function of company size. Similarly, the concept of competitive balance, in which all competitors can achieve comparable costs with differing production volumes and market shares, is also revealed to be a fallacy by the experience curve.

2.2   The Portfolio Matrix (1972)

When companies operate in various and different markets, this generally gives rise to an organisational separation into various divisions. When more and more companies started diversifying their operations in the 1970s, BCG developed a concept that was to become the basis for investment decisions for decades to come: the *Portfolio Matrix*.

The matrix, with its four subdivisions, is familiar not just to students of economics. Today, "cash cows", "dogs", "stars" and "question marks" are established elements of management talk. They describe four stages that classify operations within a company portfolio: "cash cows" stand for highly profitable, cash-generating operations based on a strong competitive position in mature markets with, if anything, fewer opportunities for growth; the "dogs" include those areas both generating below-average profits or even losses and whose markets have little potential left to tap; operations with high market share and very strong growth opportunities are known as "stars" and are the preferred candidates for investment; and finally, the "questions marks" denote operations where the market share is expanding sharply but the company's own position is weak.

2.3   Time-based Competition (1988)

In 1990, George Stalk, a BCG partner in Boston, wrote that time, used as a strategic weapon in the battle for business, had gained just as significant a position as capital, productivity, quality, and even innovation. Strategic time management made it possible for top Japanese companies to cut costs, offer wider product ranges, and increase the technical quality of their products. Rendering production more flexible made it possible to implement innovations in much shorter time and to offer a much broader variety than was conceivable for an organisation with fixed processes geared to economies of scale.

Developed in Japan in the 1980s, time-based competition overshadows to this very day many aspects of organisation-based competition: the value-creation process, and hence the ability to innovate; service quality, and hence the relationship with the customer; the relationship with suppliers, and hence a significant cost block. As the Internet increasingly enjoys more frequent and wider use, speed is becoming an increasingly important factor in many markets – victory goes to whoever is first on the market, and can thus set the standard.

How does a company become fast? By identifying and minimizing the "time-consumers" in the production processes, namely bureaucracy and the numerous interfaces in the organisation. These are found in four areas: in the organisation's throughput time – one of the reasons why business process reengineering is so attractive; in the time-to-market – nothing has such a negative effect on a product's success as a delayed launch; in the time-to-customer – mass customisation is one of the most important variants of time-based competition; and finally in the organisational structure – time-based competition becomes an ongoing challenge for the whole organisation.

2.4   Deconstruction (1997)

The "deconstruction" of the value chain is among the latest concepts developed by BCG and used successfully in the development of innovative strategies (Evans/Wurster 2000; Heuskel, 1999). This term, which originally came from literary theory and then also appeared in architecture, describes the breaking down of a whole into its constituent parts and their rebuilding to form new entities.

Two categories commonly form the framework for developing competitive strategies: the company's products or services and the industry to which it belongs, and the regional dimension of its market. In the traditional view, growth strategies concentrate on either expanding the range of products or services or on expanding the market. The company's value-creation structure, which is considered an "organisational issue," and the classification of the company to a definable industry stand outside this framework, which determines the strategic perspective.

However, these "boundaries," that have proved their validity across the decades and have shaped the strategic categories in diverse ways, are breaking down.

Whereas at the macro level, competition is forcing companies of similar structures to disaggregate and focus on individual activities, at the company level the organisation of the value chain is available for – strategic – rearrangement. In terms of strategy development, this means that a third dimension – the value chain – is being added to the two existing dimensions of product and region.

Deconstruction of the Value Chain

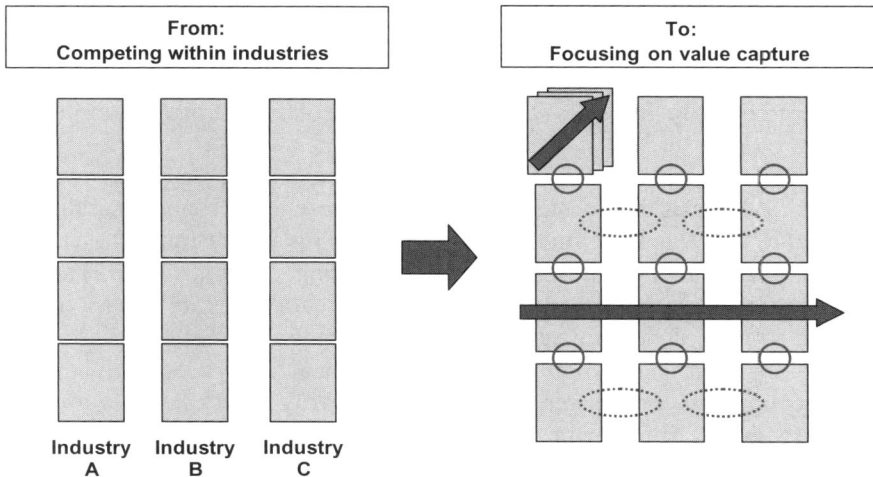

Fig. 3. Deconstruction of the value chain

Deconstruction, used actively, involves analysing value-creating activities at all levels in terms of competitiveness and in two respects: as an integrated value-creation stage and as a self-sufficient "market." Hence the logic of "outsourcing" (or "insourcing"), in the sense of entrusting value-creation activities to suppliers (or spinning off divisions), becomes a strategic decision with regard to the value-creation architecture that needs to be repeatedly reviewed, and which opens up an additional dimension for growth opportunities and innovation.

3.   Impact – From insights to results

> *"Changing an organization is inherently and inescapably*
> *an emotional human process."*

> *Jeanie Daniel Duck, Senior Vice President, BCG Los Angeles*

Concepts and strategy development form the foundation, not the objective: not until they have been implemented in the organisation and established in the company, have the changes that matter been made. In contrast to what the term perhaps traditionally implies, strategy consulting is a practical discipline, not a theoretical one.

Compared with earlier decades, the focus of consulting work has increasingly shifted from analysis and design to a more comprehensive understanding of the task at hand. As a general rule, it is no longer "just" decision options, but also results that are found at the end of the consulting concept. The organisational implementation has developed from a "downstream" task to a task integrated directly in strategy development. The requirements in terms of a consultant's skills have also changed accordingly: alongside technical expertise, a high degree of communication and conflict-resolution skills, integrity and experience are required in order to jointly implement concepts developed together at all levels of the company. Thinking and acting belong inseparably together.

Why do companies have to change? Because the ability to change is essential for survival when markets, customer demands and competitive conditions change, challenging the existing position and perspectives of the company. Adjusting existing strategic objectives, or setting new ones, is the first step in this context; the second consists of adapting the organisational reality to match these objectives. This can only happen from the inside out, and not from the outside in. To put it another way, no company will be able to change – actively – without the comprehension, willingness, skills and cooperation of the managers and staff affected, in particular with regard to common objectives. Strategic decisions will not be effective unless they have the backing of the staff in the company. Consequently, successful change projects call for much more than comprehension. They also require ongoing monitoring of the overall and intermediate targets; openness for all types of "unscheduled," disregarded and unintended collateral effects – even on a personal level; the analysis of problems that arise and a consistent orientation on interim and final results, deviations between actual and planned – which, taken together, signify a considerable burden for the entire organisation.

The Change Process

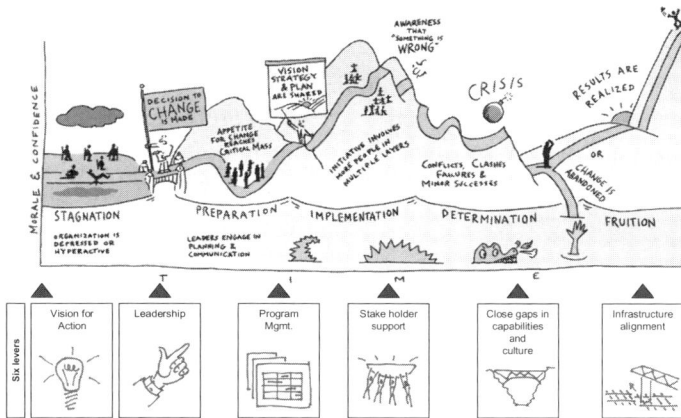

Fig. 4. The change process (Source: Duck, 2001)

Irrespective of the scope and parameters of a change project, experience indicates that three factors are essential for success: comprehension of the necessity for change and of the objectives, which feeds motivation for management and staff alike; the willingness to take leave of familiar structures and to accept new, still unknown ones; and finally, the professional and personal capabilities that may need to be acquired to accompany the changes.

In their role as external "disrupters" of an "order" that has become established over time and of a uniformity of view, consultants can initiate change processes and provide impetus for an escape from traditional patterns of thought and activity. They can, however, achieve far more than this, provided the collaborative conditions are right: they can foster the actual change process in the company at various levels.

As "externals," consultants are in a different, very advantageous position for change compared with "internals." They are neither burdened by the company's history, nor caught up in conflicts of influence and interests, and they do not need to detach themselves from familiar processes first. Their external perspective complements the internal view, hence they can communicate and integrate different positions. The balancing act that consultants have to master in change processes is how to maintain distance and independence, while working in close proximity and close cooperation.

Consultants cannot replace management in organisational implementation or take over its function. They can, however, as catalysts and communicators, moderators and mentors, coaches and controllers, accompany the company on this journey in all its stages and with all its surprises.

In practice, this means observing various perspectives and interests, and integrating them in the overall goals. Only people who can make a positive link between objectives and their own contribution will be able to make a positive contribution to change. Openness, when the targets are communicated, together with integrity and credibility when they are being implemented, are what create the trust required for people to accept change.

4.   Trust – The future of consulting

"Consulting presupposes a certain frame of mind – mental independence, the ability to swim against the tide, and the honesty only to take on those mandates that you can actually fulfill."

Bolko von Oetinger, Senior Vice President, BCG Munich

In the collaboration between consultants and clients, trust is the basis that makes the joint thinking, learning and experience process possible in the first place. Every project fosters the trust of the company, common experience promotes mutual trust. Hence it is no coincidence that long-term client relationships are the rule rather than the exception in strategy consulting. The client relationship rarely ends with the conclusion of a project. Like any relationship, it goes through phases of differing intensity.

This gives rise to what, at first, is a contradiction for the role of the consultant, between the proximity developed while collaborating over many years with mutually valued clients and the requisite distance permitting the "external view." The practical solution is found in the organisation of the consulting companies, which for the most part are structured as partnerships. Each individual shares direct responsibility for the development of the company in the form of client, experience and reputation "capital." Mastering this balancing act between individual and collective interest in client work to the benefit of both, is part and parcel of everyday consulting life. The high value placed on experience, personal maturity, independence and integrity by the consulting business is one of the main reasons behind the unusually lengthy selection and training procedures.

Trust is not just the foundation on which successful client relationships are built; it is also a successful balance within the partnership between close cooperation and ongoing knowledge transfer, and independently responsible entrepreneurship. In their training and work structures management consultancies tend to resemble the traditional "old-fashioned" structures of the manual trades.

In terms of management principles, however, they are years ahead of their time. That trust "pays off", is widely accepted today. Management based on trust and personal responsibility facilitates an intensive knowledge transfer and accelerates innovation processes. Trust creates loyalty and stability. Since productivity and value creation no longer depend (solely) on the efficient use of machinery but also on the motivation, performance and creativity of the workforce, management has less excuse for limiting itself to classical target-setting and control mechanisms.

For this reason, trust – the "third dimension" in the virtuous circle of consulting – is becoming the key factor for companies. This not only applies to the company's internal relationships, in the rapport between management and staff, but also to its external relationships with customers, shareholders and the general public. And nothing fosters this trust more than smart, logical decisions and positive results.

In this sense, the so-called "crisis of trust" has thoroughly positive effects. These days, the distinction between appearance and reality, between "stories" that create expectations and strategies that create results, is not only appreciated on the stock market. In terms of growth strategies, it has also given to rise to a new, critical scrutiny and assessment of the "truth". The same also applies to the discussion surrounding the role of the consultant and the future of this profession.

The consulting profession, in its broader sense, has a long history. Be it in the classical role of wise man or fool, or in the modern equivalent of expert or coach, it is the consultants' task to foster the decisions made by their clients on the strength of their interpretative and conceptual skills, their knowledge and their innovative ideas, in order to get closer to the "truth" together.

The functions of consultants are changing along with the expectations that industry and society have of company management in the 21st century. Just as strategy has to respond time and again to changing conditions, the role of consulting also has to be redefined time and again. The ability to innovate exists on both sides. The skill lies in being open for new developments without losing sight of the principles underlying the profession: orientation to the client, independence of thought, and integrity of action.

Consulting, conceived of as a virtuous circle of insight, impact and trust, makes "truth" a key concept for a forward-looking understanding of the consulting function. Every insight gained from perceived changes in markets, customers and economic conditions is preceded by the desire to get to the bottom of the truth, the desire to recognize the limits of your own perspective and to jointly come closer to "the truth" through interaction with others when questioning what is right. Not just in the short run, and measured by things such as a company's selling or purchase price, but with a view to its long-term, positive development.

Identifying what is right – and then doing what is right: truth, in the sense of consistent thinking and acting, is becoming the yardstick for success in consulting work. It is not potential results that count, but results actually realized – and in this context results jointly made "true."

After all, "truth" as a – repeatedly – experienced conformity between targets and results, between words and actions, between aspiration and attitude in the way consultant and client collaborate lays the foundation for trust.

It is the common search for truth to be rediscovered over and over again and its strategic translation into competitive advantages that makes the "old" profession of consulting a constantly new challenge.

References

Abegglen, James C./Stalk, George Jr. (1985): Kaisha - The Japanese Corporation. How Marketing, Money, and Manpower Strategy, Not Management Style, Make the Japanese World Pace-Setters, Perseus Books Group, New York.

Duck, Jeanie D. (2001): The Change Monster. The Human Forces that Fuel or Foil Corporate Transformation and Change, Crown Publications, New York.

Evans, Philip/Wurster, Thomas S. (2000): Blown to Bits. How the New Economics of Information Transforms Strategy, Harvard Business School Press, Boston.

Henderson, Bruce D. (1998): The Experience Curve Reviewed, in: Stern, Carl W./Stalk, George Jr.: Perspectives on Strategy from The Boston Consulting Group, John Wiley & Sons, New York, Chichester et al., pp. 12 – 14.

Heuskel, Dieter (1999): Wettbewerb jenseits von Industriegrenzen. Aufbruch zu neuen Wachstumsstrategien, Campus Fachbuch, Frankfurt/New York.

Oetinger, Bolko von (2000) (ed.): Das Boston Consulting Group Strategie-Buch. Die wichtigsten Managementkonzepte für den Praktiker, Econ, Düsseldorf.

Pierer, Heinrich von/Oetinger, Bolko von (1997): Wie kommt das Neue in die Welt?, Rowohlt, München/Wien.

Stalk, George Jr./Hout, Thomas M. (1990): Competing Against Time. How Time-Based Competition is Reshaping Global Markets, The Free Press, London/New York.

Dynamics of the Client-Consultant Relationship

Jonathan Day[1]

1. Introduction

In any discussion of consultants and consulting, we need to begin with some view of what a consultant is. My wife goes to a "beauty consultant" to have her hair done. When you buy a car, a house or an insurance policy, you speak with a "consultant." In the UK medical system, a consultant is the most senior grade of physician.

The *Oxford English Dictionary* shows uses of the term "consultant" and "consulting" from as early as 1553, when Sir Thomas Wilson wrote about "Consultyng whether the cause be profitable or unprofitable", a usage that sounds surprisingly like a modern analysis of a company's economic performance. Strategy – forward-looking analysis – appears in Shakespeare's *Richard III* (1594): "Come, gentlemen, let us consult on tomorrow's business." And C. T. Newton, in *Travels in the Levant* (1865) describes an early example of futurism: "the consultant ... sacrificed a ram, and awaited the revelations made to him in the dreams."

The terms "consultant" and "consulting" have had mixed fortunes since 1865. McKinsey, in its earliest days, presented itself as a firm of "management engineers". In his history of the consulting firm Arthur D. Little, E. J. Kahn (1986) notes that "until about the era of the Second World War, *consulting* was often a nasty word, deemed to be connected with, if not integral to, industrial espionage and like chicanery." More recently, Scott Adams, the *Dilbert* cartoonist, claims that "consult" is a combination of "con" and "insult".

In this article, I will build on my own experience both as client and as consultant, the latter not on cars or haircuts, but with general managers, mostly in very large firms. Hence I will typically use "consulting" as a shorthand for "advising general managers in large firms on management issues." I will also draw on interviews that my firm has conducted; these involved both clients and non-clients of McKinsey.[2]

While my own firm, McKinsey, has shaped my perspectives, the title of this series is not "quo vadis McKinsey" but "quo vadis consulting", and I will say relatively little about McKinsey itself. I should add, for the avoidance of doubt,

---

[1] I am grateful to Matthew Robb for helpful discussion and research in the preparation of this paper, and to Paul Coombes, Tony Danker, Ansgar Richter, John Roberts and James Wendler for comments on earlier drafts.

[2] When no source is provided, quoted comments are from interviews conducted by current and former colleagues. Names and identifying details have been eliminated.

that the perspectives set forth here are my own and do not necessarily reflect the views of McKinsey & Company.

In what follows, I will discuss the evolution of the client-consultant relationship: its setting, the ways in which consultants seek to add value to their clients, and the ways in which consultant and client seek to manage the relationship. I will close with some thoughts on the future of the profession.

2.   The setting of the client-consultant relationship

Management consulting takes place in different forms and settings. A large consultancy such as McKinsey generally serves a company rather than an individual, and the services are typically rendered by the consultancy as a whole – visible to the client as a team, but often drawing on resources from around the world – rather than by an individual consultant. But many combinations appear in practice: one individual advising another; an individual practitioner advising a company; occasionally, a firm of consultants advising an individual executive.

At times, one sort of relationship will be embedded in another. In the course of a large firm advising a particular company, an individual consultant – a member of the consultancy, but for the moment acting as an individual – could provide coaching or counsel to a particular executive in the company. A tension can arise between the necessary confidentiality of a one-to-one meeting and the legitimate desires of the leaders of the two institutions – the CEO of the client and the supervising partner in the consultancy – to know what is going on.

Companies that do use consultants will frequently employ more than one at a time. A firm of consultants can work across an organisation, gathering data and discussing recommendations with more managers than an individual. Yet an independent practitioner, not affiliated with a large firm and thus unencumbered by its client development agenda, can often build strong counselling relationships, sometimes spanning many years. The interactions of consulting firms and sole practitioners, both serving the same client, can lead to interesting (and sometimes difficult) outcomes.

Another element of the setting of the client-consultant relationship involves the client's purpose in engaging the consultant. Ideally, the client seeks nothing other than the best outcome for his organisation. If the consultant recommends closing the division that the client happens to lead, the recommendation will be followed if it is genuinely best for the company.

In most cases I have experienced, both client and consultant seek the greater good of the client's company. But it is rare to find absolutely undivided and dispassionate commitment to this objective. Even the most dedicated corporate executive will have some personal interest both in the process of a consulting project and in its outcome. In some cases, managers see consultants as conduits to the most senior management of the company, or as means for enhancing the manager's personal reputation. At times, consultants can be imposed on a manager by superiors in the company, and the consulting relationship can be driven by fear. Some managers hire consultants to justify decisions they have already taken.

Equally, while consultants should strive for independence and eschew personal motives in seeking and accepting assignments, these ideals are difficult to attain. A consulting firm's ethos and policies should make it easy for any consultant to refuse an assignment that is not likely to add value to the client company. Yet even in such an environment, consultants can feel pressure to affirm the quality of relationships through continued client activity or to help an executive, even when it appears that the executive's company will derive little tangible benefit.

Since some ulterior considerations play a role in most consulting assignments, principled clients and consultants are frequently faced with deciding whether, despite personal motives, the benefit of a potential project is worth the risk of its being subverted to serve private ends. During the course of an assignment, and especially at points of decision as to whether or not to extend its duration, private objectives need to be checked and discussed. What sounds like a simple relationship – a client who wants advice for the good of the company, and a consultant who provides that advice in a disinterested and objective way – can become tricky to navigate.

3.   Levels of value added

I will return to the discussion of the setting of the relationship. First, though, I would like to examine the kind of services that a consultant can provide a client, and the value added by each service. Broadly speaking, we can array the services that can be provided along a hierarchy of levels of added value. The framework that follows is derived from *The Experience Economy*, by Joseph Pine and James Gilmore (1999).

1. At a very basic level, consultants can provide **data**: what was McDonalds' market share for hamburgers in South London during 2003? What were Shell's oil reserves in Nigeria at the start of 2001? What sorts of chewing gum do 10- to 12-year old middle class girls in Paris prefer? In some cases, providing data is primarily a matter of exploiting the consultant's scale and its ability to organise production and distribution – for example, sending researchers out to collect information from public filings. In others, considerable expertise is needed to sift through data and deliver accurate results. As suggested by the Shell example, accurate data can drastically affect the fortunes of a firm. With few exceptions, though, providing data alone requires relatively little interaction with the client, other than to specify what is needed.

2. Moving up a level of value added, data can be incorporated into a package, a **product**. When this happens, the data becomes endowed with interpretation and purpose. The Economist Intelligence Unit, for example offers packaged reports on 200 countries, not only providing detailed data but also summarising key economic and political trends, providing overviews of political and economic structure, analysing recent trends and offering an outlook for political

and economic prospects.[3] A product can lead to changes in a client, and hence can be a form of management consultancy. The numerous "how to" business books sold in airport bookstalls contain recommendations and specific instructions. But, like a cookbook, a product is generic. The EIU will sell a country profile on Argentina to anyone prepared to pay the price – $265 as I write this. There is almost no interaction between client and consultant at this level.

3. A product can be adapted to a client's specific situation, and provided in an interactive way; this is a **service.** Much of management consulting is about adapting a consultant's knowledge (data, product) to the circumstances of the client, and such a service can be delivered in a fairly pedestrian way. You may or may not remember the last conversation you had with your "beauty consultant" or "dental hygiene consultant". Highly interactive software can blur the line between products and services. An interactive corporate survey, for example, might adapt the questions it poses based on a respondent's previous answers, as well as delivering highly customised feedback to each respondent. Even where standardised products are offered, consultants often provide process orchestration, leading the client through interviews, workshops and the like.

4. Though some services are unmemorable, others can be highly engaging. Many of the services of a top law firm, investment bank or strategy consultancy are often endowed with high drama; they become not just a matter of calculating market shares or solving technical problems but of setting the course of entire firms, reshaping industries or creating new possibilities for millions of customers. The design of professional offices, the style of client communications, the elaborate disclaimers and notices of secrecy attached to documents all have practical justifications, but also change services into **experiences**. These supposedly minor features of the consulting process help add an element of seriousness and drama to a project.

Pine and Gilmore describe the lowest level, which I have called data, as a commodity: "Commodities are fungible, services are intangible, experiences are memorable." The engaging, memorable element of an experience enhances the likelihood that the client will remember and implement recommendations. They set out the levels in a hierarchy, an adapted version of which appears in figure 1.

---

[3] See their website, www.eiu.com, for detailed product and pricing information.

Sources of Added Value

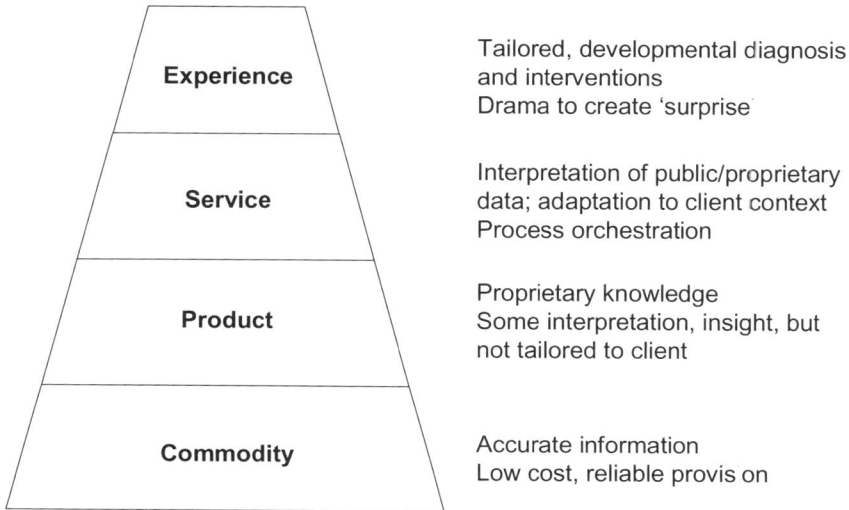

Experience	Tailored, developmental diagnosis and interventions Drama to create 'surprise'
Service	Interpretation of public/proprietary data; adaptation to client context Process orchestration
Product	Proprietary knowledge Some interpretation, insight, but not tailored to client
Commodity	Accurate information Low cost, reliable provis on

Fig. 1. Sources of added value

We can apply the framework to the task of decorating a room. The titanium dioxide used to make paint white is a commodity. TiO_2 in a base with specific usage characteristics (gloss, water resistance, etc.) is a product. The painters who apply the paint, figuring out how to avoid damaging exposed woodwork, are providing a service. And the interior designer who works with the client to create a "look" reflecting a specific personality and lifestyle, may well do so in an engaging, memorable way.

Most large-scale consulting assignments work across the spectrum from commodity to experience. A strategy assignment will typically draw on a great deal of data; it may incorporate generic analyses or models (products); it will certainly adapt both data gathering and the framing of recommendations to the specifics of the client (services). If the goal of the engagement is to produce a report that sits on the client's shelf, no more is needed.

But skilled consultants typically hope that their work will lead to action and change in the client, and hence will develop strategy in an interactive way, often involving client managers as members of the consulting team, holding extensive workshops and off-site meetings, and seeking to make the process memorable – to convert a service into an experience. Consultants speak of the need for client "ownership" of their recommendations and of the value of skill transfer; these statements are true, but a good part of the language, style and process of top consulting firms is focused on creating excitement and drama, both for the clients and for the consultants involved.

In many consulting firms and consulting assignments, the four levels of added value are delivered simultaneously. Although consulting assignments often begin with data collection and end with some process of client engagement, it would be unusual for the consultants to construct a separate phase in which "experience" is added to the basic service. Experiential elements typically enter an assignment on its first day, as the consulting team members begin to work with their client counterparts.

4.   The client's perspective

Corporate executives have become more sophisticated and thoughtful in the ways in which they hire management consultants. In many cases, they specify where on the hierarchy they are seeking assistance. The strategy director of an energy company said, in an interview:

> "We are not looking for general business advice. We have sufficient capacity internally to do that. We have employed consultants to do a study of the potential of particular markets that we would like to go into. Their technical, commercial and analytical expertise is what is valued most in the organisation. It is more specific knowledge and expertise that we would like to buy, and less process."

This executive clearly states that he doesn't want much adaptation to his company's situation. Of course there will be tailoring, but relatively little process orchestration. In the framework set out above, this company wants consultants to provide a product, or at most a highly structured service.

The same executive noted that,

> "What has also worked well is when we have really specified very clear boundaries / scope. Consultants are very opportunistic and they will quickly seek to fill gaps."

This quote illustrates a general pattern: some clients seek to "commoditise" consulting, by unbundling it, turning experiences into services and services into products. They try to work downward in the hierarchy while consultants have a natural tendency to push upward.

Yet the pressure to move down in the hierarchy is not universal. Here is a leading management academic speaking about his own consulting practice.

> "Top management in global companies see a lot of value in the integration of 'content' and 'facilitation' from their advisors. The management team has to have deep involvement in the development of strategy because that builds skill and ownership and insight. My own consulting practice is built around this. I spend two to five days with my clients, it's a mixture of education, debate, decision-making, and a lot of fun. I cannot begin to meet the demand for my services in this area. ... A good content-based facilitator needs to be a good teacher and also a good entertainer."

Similar phenomena appear in fields other than management consulting. Pine and Gilmore cite an article in the medical journal *The Lancet*, in which two Canadian physicians wrote that

> If a physician does not possess the necessary skills to assess a patient's emotional needs and to display clear and effective responses to those needs, the job is not done. Consequently, we believe that medical training should include an acting curriculum, focused on the conveying of appropriate, beneficial responses to those emotional needs.
>
> In my practice ... I frequently treat individuals who are in chronic pain. I find it essential to convey an encouraging, hopeful, often cajoling message to the patient, to communicate concern and, more importantly, the need for the patient to work on self-improvement (Finestone/Conter, 1994, p. 801).

The article generated considerable controversy, with many doctors insisting that their roles were purely technical. Other doctors noted that a positive patient experience led to more disclosure from patients, and hence better diagnosis, better compliance with treatments, and fewer lawsuits. Experienced management consultants are well aware that a positive, engaging experience typically leads to richer information from the client, earlier disclosure of issues that could impede implementation and a higher likelihood of the client following the consultant's recommendations. Early in my career in McKinsey, a partner admonished me, "You are on stage at every moment of your working day. You can't forget that for a second."

The term *acting*, as used by Finestone, Conter, Pine and Gilmore, can be misinterpreted as manipulation, bringing to mind George Burns's dictum: "The most important thing in acting is honesty. If you can fake that, you've got it made." This, I believe, is an error. The "acting" that goes on in the consulting room of a skilled physician does not cover up technical competences that the physician does not hold; similarly, a management consultant who is also an "actor" is not attempting to deceive the client. In both cases, the professional is seeking to leave the client with deeply felt and hence actionable knowledge about physical or economic health. The "acting" described here is closer to a saying of Marlon Brando's: "Nobody 'becomes' a character. You can't act unless you are who you are."

5.   Roles within the client-consultant relationship

Ideally, client and consultant will agree on the role that each will play within the relationship.

- If the consultant's primary role is as a provider of data, the client takes the role of a skilled procurement manager: specifying, with precision, the commodity to be provided; ensuring that the consultant's offer is tested against market alternatives; selecting the consultant; and then doing everything possible to ensure that the data can be gathered and transmitted efficiently – for example, ensuring that internal issues do not block the completion of surveys or interviews, or making company records available. The consultant plays the role of supplier: ensuring that there is a clear understanding of what is to be provided, proposing commercial terms that will attract the client, and supplying the requisite data as quickly as possible. In many cases consultants who find themselves in this role would do well to resist the temptation to push for greater added value. Executives who are concerned about consultants "seeking to fill gaps" will appreciate the consultant who provides the requisite data and then steps out of the way.

- The relationship changes where the data is embedded within a product. Here, the relationship revolves around product selection. The consultant and client need to ensure that the purpose for which the product is sought is mutually understood and that the product is in fact fit for that purpose. It is rarely in a consultant's interest – and never in the client's – to sell a product that cannot deliver the improved performance that the client seeks. Yet the pressures to increase volume can be overwhelming. Many product salesforces, such as those selling ERP software, seek to adopt what is sometimes called "consultative selling", meaning that salespeople are discouraged from pushing products that are not in the client's interest. Yet these objectives are hard to sustain: incentives, culture, the client's expectations and individual sales consultants' backgrounds can all interfere with the right questions being asked and answered. Sales groups that seek to adopt such a consultative approach often have to go through extensive change, both in incentive systems and in fundamental culture.

- Where a true service is involved, the role metaphor shifts toward that of a *patient and a clinician*. Here, client and consultant need to engage in a programme of diagnosis before any solutions can be offered. In management settings, even the symptoms of a problem can be elusive. One chief executive opened a conversation by saying, "I feel I am swimming in treacle. What can you do about that?" Considerable interaction may be needed to understand the problem that the client perceives, to clarify what is really going on and to develop a range of solutions. It is essential that both participants resist cutting the process short, jumping to solutions before developing a complete understanding of the problem, or settling for solutions whose need and purpose are not clearly understood.
When the consultant's offer moves from product to service, both client and consultant must begin to distinguish between service to the individual from service to the overall organisation. In the above example, some consultants might work with the executive about his feelings of "swimming in treacle" and explore what he can do, apart from any change in the organisation, to operate more effectively. Other consultants would focus on the organisation itself, and the structures and behaviours that contribute to the "treacle".

- The boundary between service and experience can be tenuous, as suggested by the Canadian doctors quoted above. But when an experiential relationship (or, as more commonly described, an "engaging" one) is sought by client and consultant, the roles can be similar to those of an *athlete and a coach*. The consultant's role is to build an understanding of the client's level of development and potential to develop further, then to challenge and help the client to move on to higher levels. Frequent, substantial interaction will be needed; some of this may at times seem fruitless. Such a relationship is risky for both consultant and client; it requires patience and mutual trust in a way that a cut-and-dried service does not. It is also essential, in such a relationship, for consultant and client to agree, before the fact, on the focus of the work given that the "athlete" in question can be an individual client or the client's organisation.

The pyramid of added value also suggests methods for testing the quality of a particular consulting assignment.

- For commodity consulting, the primary test is of *conformity to specification*. Are the share figures truly reflective of market realities? Have the requisite employees been surveyed? Have appropriate geological and geophysical tests been done to verify oil reserve figures?

- A product is typically tested by its *fitness for purpose*: does the new accounting system produce a monthly close within three days? Did the audience find the lecture interesting and useful? Did the generic training programme in fact impart the desired skills?

- Services require *adaptation to the client's context*: did the tailored training programme take account of an individual division's special circumstances? Was the customer segmentation project completed with a good understanding of the company's existing customer base?

- An experiential process is tested by the *quality of engagement* that it fosters. Did the client find the process surprising? Exciting? Did the project create a sense of energy and drama within the client organisation? Was it seen as a pivotal event in the client company's development?

It would be easy to conclude from this discussion that the higher levels of value added are somehow "better" than the lower ones. This is not the case. "Commodity" or "product" consulting can be very profitable for its providers, and more welcomed by some clients than service or experiential work. All four kinds of consulting can be difficult to do well. All can contribute to a firm's success, and a skilled client will initiate projects that draw from the full spectrum of added value.

A few generalisations can be made, however. The ability of the parties to contract diminishes as the relationship moves from commodity to experience. Where a third party can be engaged to verify that data conforms to specification, or even that a product was fit for purpose, service- or experience- based consulting is harder to evaluate in this way. The need for rich interaction also increases, both in the sourcing of consulting work and in its delivery. Data and products can be purchased over the internet, and some corporations are procuring basic legal services (a "services" purchase) via internet auction. But experiential, engaging work requires the consultant's presence and an open door to the client's office: it is sometimes described as a "contact sport".

6.   Development of the consulting profession

The value added framework may also be helpful in making sense of the development of consulting as an industry or profession. Space allows for only a cursory sketch here.

The consulting that emerged in the early 1900s was solution-based – in a certain sense, these were products: time-and-motion and 'scientific management' practitioners such as Frederick Winslow Taylor, Frank Gilbreth and Edwin Booz offered "management engineering" services and specific practices that could be moved from plant to plant or firm to firm with some ease.

The late 1920s and 1930s saw the beginnings of more systemic views of firms and their management, with thinkers such as Chester Barnard and Alfred P. Sloan. James Oscar McKinsey, the founder of my firm, started as a professor of accountancy, and his early published work was on budgeting systems – by today's standards, closer to the "product" category. As he developed McKinsey & Company, he shifted toward a more systemic view of his clients, promulgating a survey outline that required consultants to understand a wide range of aspects of a firm and its business environment and insisting that his clients allow consultants to gather facts from across a company.

Marvin Bower, who succeeded James O. McKinsey as the firm's leader and presided over its development for many years, completed the shift from products to experiential consulting. Bower viewed consulting as a profession rather than an industry and sought to endow it with the style and rhetoric of a law firm. He is famous for insisting on stringent standards of dress and deportment for his consultants, and on prescribing the language to be used in speaking about clients, the firm and its work. Bower's influence spread well beyond McKinsey.

More recent years have, arguably, seen pressure to push downward in the pyramid, as large corporations have sought to reduce consulting costs. Formal invitations to tender are more common nowadays, as are procurement managers dedicated to sourcing consulting services. Some of the mystique surrounding consultants and consulting has been eroded as the profession has grown. While experiential, engaging consulting is still practiced, it can conflict with the procurement agent's desire to specify outcomes and deliverables with precision and to restrict the consultant's scope of enquiry and action.

7.   A higher level of value added

I have presented a four-level hierarchy: commodities, products, services and experiences. Gilmore and Pine add a fifth, which they term "transformation". By this, they mean that the process changes the client. But that is true for the best experiential work, and change can occur at far lower levels. A revelation of previously unknown data, for example, can bring about substantial change within a client.

Beyond this, the term "transformation" has been used by consultants in a way similar to the re-engineering programmes of the 1980s, to describe large scale, multi-faceted change programmes. In the framework I have suggested, these are best put in the "experience" category: the consultant not only provides substantial process orchestration ("services") but also tends to create dramatic episodes through workshops and similar group encounters.

But there is another level of transformation that can occur when clients and consultants work together. It is a deeper transformation, a change in the client's collective awareness and perspective. This deep transformation is often more powerful because it is unconscious and because it can be difficult to identify a particular point at which the change occurred; as the academic and consultant Patricia Shaw puts it, these are collective "changes in the conversation" (Shaw, 2002). Such changes can occur within consumer markets, as for example when Swatch watches or the Harry Potter stories suddenly occupied large parts of the consumer landscape; in the world of politics, when there is a "revolution" in thinking, as with the sudden increase in public attention to privatisation, markets and competition during the Thatcher years in Britain. And it can occur within corporate leaders, teams and entire companies, as firms change their views of the markets they compete in, the businesses they are operating and the ways in which they work.

A board member of a global oil company described such a shift in collective consciousness. The company experimented with a variety of organisational approaches for matching business unit entrepreneurship with strong firmwide controls on policy areas such as finance, reputation, ethics and people. The eventual solution emerged in multiple settings; suddenly, executives discovered that

> "... you could design things so you weren't limited by any single structure. You could design the way interactions happened according to what you wanted to achieve. That is a very liberating thought. It lets you step outside ways of running the company that are limited by conventional models of structure. It begins to allow you to have different structures depending on what you are doing."

I have called this fifth level of value added *metanoia*, a term derived from the Greek *meta*, beyond, and *noiein* or *nous*, thinking or thought. Metanoia occurs throughout the New Testament and is sometimes translated in English as "repentance", but in fact it best describes the experience that St Paul had on the Damascus Road. We could contrast "transformation" – from the Latin *transformare*, a change in form or shape – with the Greek *metanoia*, a change in mind, typically, a change to a higher plane. Figure 2 completes the pyramid and the spectrum of consulting approaches – and relationships – from data to *metanoia.*

Completing the Pyramid

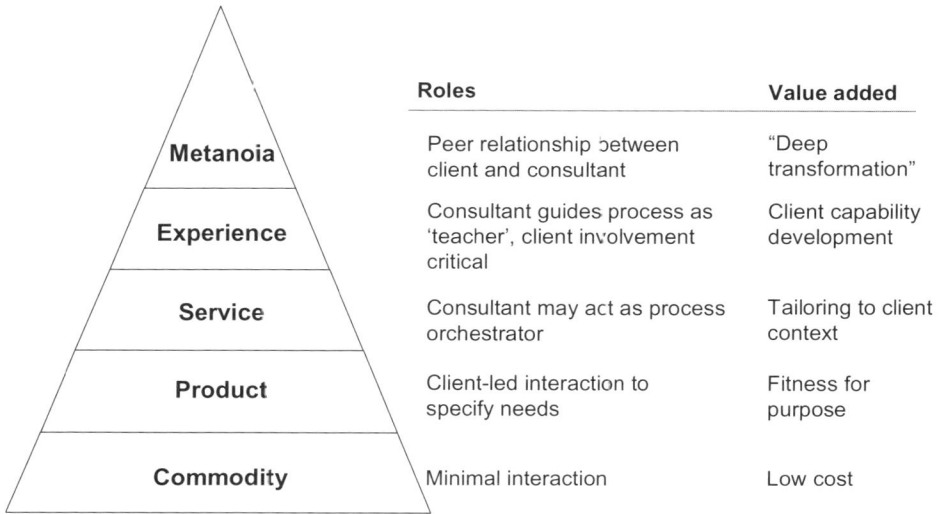

	Roles	Value added
Metanoia	Peer relationship between client and consultant	"Deep transformation"
Experience	Consultant guides process as 'teacher', client involvement critical	Client capability development
Service	Consultant may act as process orchestrator	Tailoring to client context
Product	Client-led interaction to specify needs	Fitness for purpose
Commodity	Minimal interaction	Low cost

Fig. 2. Completing the pyramid

Consulting aimed at bringing about *metanoia* is fundamentally difficult, largely because the change in mind to be achieved can never be precisely specified in advance. There is no "from-to" at this level; at best there are ideas about what can be done and where the client company should go, but these ideas become material for debate rather than a rhetorical agenda that the consultant hopes to impose on the client. Consulting for *metanoia* is focused on dialogue rather than "buy in". It therefore requires a peer relationship between client and consultant. At this level there is true partnership, a degree of intimacy, and mutual development. Returning to the role metaphors outlined above, *teacher and student* may apply, but it can be difficult, observing these interactions from the outside, to know which party is the teacher and which the student. When this happens, the consultants learn from the clients as much as the other way around. When transformation occurs, it feels like discovery, both on the client's part and on the consultant's. It is, as a result, typically far longer-lasting: the client has not "bought into" the consultant's idea, but rather created a new set of possibilities in partnership with the consultant. One CEO put it this way:

> "The natural aspects of the old leadership don't work anymore. It is not just a question of saying that I need to communicate more. I need to really transform myself in a way that is almost unnatural because it changes the very essence of everything for which I trained or what I had been told and understood in the beginning."

Just as it is difficult to specify the outcome of this fifth-level consulting, it is challenging to script or plan interactions between consultant and client. Some of the most effective consultants I know, in McKinsey and elsewhere, prepare extensively for client interactions of this sort but discard all of their notes and exhibits before entering the client's office. This work is far more like improvisational drama or jazz than like a Shakespeare play or a symphony. The conversation takes unexpected turns. It is hard to plan, impossible to manage to targets. One simply cannot say, "by next Tuesday, you must have formed an intimate relationship with client X."

New consultants in the mainstream firms are typically taught to form a hypothesis about "the answer" to the client's problem and to be ready to convey this answer to the CEO, just in case CEO and consultant happen to meet in the company elevator. For those skilled in analytic problem solving, hypothesis formation and the crisp and powerful communication of "the answer" – one has, after all, only the length of the elevator ride to get the message across – consulting for *metanoia* can be frightening and difficult. It requires the ability simultaneously to hold an objective in mind and to suspend that goal so that a superior solution can emerge. Robert Kegan, the developmental psychologist, describes a point in adult development in which an individual is capable not only of having a world view but also of objectifying this view, "holding but not being held by" a perspective. This "interinstitutional" standpoint, in Kegan's terms, is essential for the consultant who wishes to work toward *metanoia*.[4]

8.   Outlook for consulting and consulting firms

There are individual consultants and consulting firms that claim to work at the *metanoia* level, though they tend to use the term "transformation". Most use a variety of psychological techniques and group processes. Some claim to be able to bring about deep transformation in a predictable, reliable manner. In most cases, these consultants rely on their clients to define the direction in which they move: they often say that they have "no agenda" other than achieving what the client seeks. They are often effective coaches and facilitators, but, lacking knowledge of the underlying business and its economics, it is difficult to see how they can function at the peer level that I have outlined above.

Most of the larger consulting firms will continue to work at the level of service and experience. Scale works against moving upward in the hierarchy, because scale inevitably requires a degree of standardisation and a move toward packages. Beyond this, the major firms are in the business of offering clients "solutions"; seen at one level, this requires standing outside the client's world and proposing a direction in which change should take place, identifying the move "from" one state today "to" another tomorrow. This sort of consulting can add a lot of value; it

---

[4] Kegan (1998) posits five levels of adult development, which roughly correspond to the five levels of value added I have set out above.

is not necessarily inferior to the mutual discovery involved in *metanoia*, but it is fundamentally different.

Equally, we can expect to see continuing pressure from clients to move down the hierarchy. Clients will ask their consultants to provide smaller, more modular service packages, and to deliver products electronically rather than interactively, where this can be done without too much loss of value.

The space at the top of the hierarchy remains alluring, both because the experience of consulting at this level can be highly satisfying for consultant and client and because the changes that such work can bring about within clients can be deep and lasting. Intuitively, it should be possible for consultants both to develop a strong point of view on issues of strategy, organisation or operations and to suspend that point of view in a creative dialogue with their clients, a dialogue in which *metanoia* might systematically occur.

Many of the major firms – McKinsey included – are experimenting with the pre-conditions in which this *might* happen, but none seems to have found reliable and predictable ways to achieve it. This highest level of value added seems to be a bit like the problem of reliably growing truffles: we can observe and replicate all of the external conditions (oak trees, soil, etc.) but we cannot force the outcome. The old parable still holds:

> "...the kingdom of heaven is like unto a merchant, seeking goodly pearls: Who, when he had found one pearl of great price, went and sold all that he had, and bought it." (Matthew 13.45)

The views expressed in this chapter are those of the author and not necessarily of McKinsey & Company.

References

Finestone, Hillel M./Conter, David (1994): Acting in Medical Practice, in: The Lancet, Vol. 344, No. 8925, 17 September 1994.

Kahn, Ely J. Jr. (1986): The Problem Solvers: A History of Arthur D. Little, Inc., Little Brown, Boston.

Kegan, Robert (1998): In Over Our Heads: The Mental Demands of Modern Life, Belknap Press, Boston.

Pine, Joseph B./Gilmore, James H. (1999): The Experience Economy, Harvard Business School Press, Boston.

Shaw, Patricia (2002): Changing Conversations in Organizations, Routledge, London.

From Exchangeable Methods to Implementable Results – The Utilization of Tools and Solution Competencies in Strategy Consulting

Franz-Josef Seidensticker

1. Management methods: From trademark to tool kit

Are there any executives out there who are still talking about Lean Management, TQM (Total Quality Management), or Business Re-engineering? And yet, these productivity enhancing methods were once as popular as CRM (Customer Relationship Management) or the often misunderstood and misused concept of Shareholder Value have been over the past few years.

Management methods are a favourite target for criticism, because the approaches and concepts spread in a similar manner through imitation and frequently with considerable assistance from the media – only to fade away without so much as a whimper, or so it would seem. Management consultants are often accused of creating or inflating these method-fads, and using them for their own marketing purposes or as a way to create work for themselves. At least, that is, until difficulties arise with these originally celebrated recipes for success and it becomes apparent that they are not panaceas. Then, logic would dictate, it is suddenly high time for the consultants to turn to the next best problem, whether acute or latent, and promptly concoct, label and market a solution so that this profitable game can begin anew.

As with any caricature, there is a grain of truth in this depiction of the way methods are utilized by management consultants. Consultants, like everyone, operate in competition. They, too, must convince clients of the quality of their product – which means, above all, their competence. The best measure of this, of course, has always been the proven usefulness of the firm's past projects. At the same time, a consulting firm, like any enterprising company, also wants its achievements to be recognized by the general public.

Since it is impossible to directly compare competence, the contest of ideas remains. A consulting firm can best show its dedication to finding new ways to benefit clients by calling attention to the fresh perspectives, new insights and, yes, new methods that it has discovered or created in the course of its consulting work. In general, the fact that such know-how can be used for marketing purposes is usually just a pleasant side effect.

Method innovation played a particularly important differentiating role as a Unique Selling Proposition (USP) in the early days of management consulting (Ming 2001). For instance, Overhead Value Analysis (OVA) opened the door for the international expansion of McKinsey & Company, eventually developing into a trademark of the firm. Companies that greatly expanded in the period following World War Two had built up an overcapacity of personnel, especially in the area of administration. The OVA method offered a systematic approach to quantifying cost-cutting potential, localizing it and formulating specific measures for implementation.

Similarly, the rapid spread of another famous consulting product, Strategic Portfolio Analysis, was not based simply on the clear understandability of the BCG Portfolio Matrix, with its four catchy-named categories: "Cash cows"; "Stars"; "Question marks"; and "Dogs". This method, developed by the Boston Consulting Group founder Bruce Henderson, also promised a solution to prevailing problems. The diversification policy pursued by many companies – sometimes in the form of aggressive acquisitions – had begun to reach its limits. Bad deals were piling up, putting substantial strain on financial and personnel resources. In many cases, it was next to impossible to keep track and control of the expanded variety of a company's business activities. With the help of Portfolio Analysis, it was possible to evaluate business areas according to their appeal and the volume of investment required, in order to derive recommendations for the allocation of funding to the individual businesses as well as to eliminate unattractive areas.

The extent of the Portfolio Analysis method's usefulness is not only demonstrated by the rapidity with which the consulting community adopted it, but can also be seen in the various improvements and further developments made to the original, now more critically regarded Market Growth – Market Share approach. And though *The* portfolio approach, as an independent strategy formula, no longer exists today, specific portfolio analyses remain indispensable as part of the Strategic Management Consulting tool kit.

Later method-fads, such as Lean Management, Business Process Re-engineering or the CRM movement cannot be attributed solely to the activities of self-proclaimed or media-styled management gurus either. Nor were they just the result of marketing by others, e.g. from the IT sector, which likes to sell management concepts as ready-made software solutions. Closer consideration clearly demonstrates that new methods have always resonated best when they were able to meet the needs of a large number of companies for simpler, faster or more efficient solutions to serious problems.

For example, the idea of Total Quality Management (TQM), based on the pioneering work of the American statistician and management theorist W. Edwards Deming, served to help the Japanese economy back on to its feet in the 1950's. However, it was much later, when Japanese electronics and automobile manufacturers were making definite strides internationally thanks to the "zero defects" philosophy, that companies and consultants in the West began to sit up and take notice of Deming's work. Customer Relationship Management (CRM) has similarly gained in popularity to the extent that the loyalties of an ever better informed and aggressively solicited clientele have begun to unravel.

Companies are often under pressure to take action, which naturally promotes the tendency to overestimate the usefulness or universality of individual management methods. In many cases, key factors regarding applicability and successful implementation are overlooked – especially when the likes of software providers promise an immediately functional solution at the touch of a button. As empirical studies have shown time and again, the massive deployment of information technology is, in itself, no guarantee of success. Failure is more often than not the result of decisions made to implement a certain IT solution before the fundamental strategic and organizational issues have been adequately considered.

Taking CRM as an example, this means that careful segmenting must first be done to identify the type of client it would be most advantageous to win and keep. The next step is to discern the needs and wants of these valuable clients and to measure their degree of satisfaction and loyalty in order to find a basis for specific actions. The extent to which internal structures, systems and processes should be adjusted to allow greater customer orientation must also be examined. Only after all of this has been done, can questions be answered as to which processes should be automated and to what degree. Consequently, the choice of suitable hardware and software is the last step in the process.

The preceding example also shows that the days are over in which a management approach could be encompassed and comprehended in a simple analysis scheme such as the BCG Portfolio Matrix. Today, abbreviations like CRM or SCM (Supply Chain Management) stand for complex concepts, comprising several levels and dimensions of analysis, and requiring the employment of a wide variety of methods.

On the other hand, there has been an increase in the level of knowledge concerning the reach and limitations of management methods for consultants and companies. Both sides have gathered and learned from experience. The companies have grown more critical, and in general, leaders in management consulting no longer tout their method innovations. Rather, consultants prove their problem-solving competencies by showcasing their excellent personnel qualifications and their great expertise in specific areas. Several management concepts and analysis tools are now common knowledge anyway, so that their standard usage lends little or no advantage in problem solving or competition.

Growing experience using a new method, however, can elevate the incidence of success significantly. An example of this is shown in the results of a worldwide survey on the use of management tools, conducted annually by Bain & Company since 1993. In 2000, only 35 percent of the 708 companies surveyed used CRM. The proportion of those who had stopped using the method due to disappointment (defection rate) was 18 percent. Two years later, in 2002, twice as many companies were using CRM. The degree of user satisfaction had also increased significantly, and the defection rate was down to only 3 percent (Rigby 2003).

In general, the results of the management tool surveys from past years show that the companies make choices based on the prevailing situation. They regard the arsenal of available methods as a tool kit, from which they can select the tools they consider to be most suitable to meet the acute challenges they face in the light of their evaluation of the prevailing competitive environment and business outlook.

In 2002, for instance, the focus around the globe once again emphasized instruments for exploiting growth potential more strongly than cost-cutting tools.

At the same time, however, the companies took care to exercise discipline. The tendency was to use proven methods for planning and controlling that would help in averting uncontrolled expansion. By way of contrast, instruments that required large outlays of cash or served to divert the attention of managers from the companies' core business (e.g. share buybacks, corporate venturing or acquisitions) were less widely used.

Geographical and size differences also play a role in the tool selection. For example, expansion was a more important issue for Asian companies than for North American or European competitors, who were, in turn, more concerned with cost cutting than their Asian rivals. The management of mid-sized enterprises concentrated more frequently on growth than larger companies did, and was more concerned with avoiding layoffs.

2.   Method know-how in consulting

The business challenges that companies decide to undertake, and in which areas they see a particular need for action is also reflected in the demand for specific consulting themes and concepts. According to a new Fink study (2004), the top priorities of German companies for both the short and medium term – until 2008 – are focused on Business Process Re-engineering and Lean Management, methods aimed at increasing productivity and cutting costs. For the short term, growth strategies and CRM, approaches for developing new clients and capitalizing on existing ones and turnover potential, rank only third or fourth.

On the one hand, this reflects a problem of doing business in Germany, which is exposed to increasing cost competition, mainly from Asia. On the other hand, the defensive stance taken by companies, shown by the fact that growth strategies slide as far down in the ranking to the 7th position for 2008, is disconcerting.

It is evident that companies are preparing for difficult times from the criteria they consider most important when choosing a consultant. Even though the functionality of the solution still tops the list, the ranking of the criteria thereafter has shifted in comparison to 2002. Two years ago, the ability to communicate, transfer of know-how, and social competence ranked above method and industry expertise, placed only fifth and sixth on the list. Now these two capabilities, which are key to accurate diagnosis and the quality of the solution, have moved up to second and third place – followed by sector-specific know-how, appearing in the ranking for the first time.

The higher significance placed by the clients today on the method competence of the consultant cannot be attributed to a revival of a naive belief in methods. On the contrary, companies know from experience how important the intelligent use of methods is for the success of the consulting process, but they realize, too, that a high level of expertise is necessary for correct method selection and application.

Consultants are expected to stay abreast of the newest method developments. This entails recruiting the most gifted individuals from universities, who bring with them the most up-to-date knowledge available. The management of a company cannot spend time on this, if it does not want to neglect its core tasks. This realization most likely contributed to fact that the transfer of know-how has lost importance as selection criteria for a consultant. Additionally, know-how can quickly become obsolete – not because it is fundamentally outdated, but because the situation of the company undergoes changes or because new methods are better suited in certain instances. Method competence therefore comprises more than a formal mastery of tools for problem diagnosis and structuring. Generation and evaluation of alternative solutions, execution and measurement of success, sound formal knowledge of methods, the how-to-do, are all part of the basic precondition for professional consulting work.

A key factor in consulting success is further reaching knowledge about the performance and efficiency of the methods available. Within which scope can they be applied – i.e. in terms of problem categories, sectors, company functions, observation levels or phases of the consulting process? What strengths and weaknesses does a method have? How reliable are the results? What problems could occur – e.g. in data collection? Which obstacles should be watched out for – e.g. when interpreting results? How involved is a method? Is the intervention effective in cost-benefit terms or would a more robust approach provide equally useful insights? Which methods are best suited to particular areas? What is the optimum combination of methods in a specific case?

It is a constant learning process to know when and where to employ a particular method. In their work consultants are continuously confronted with different markets and companies, structures and behaviour patterns. The relevance of implemented methods is therefore repeatedly tested under differing conditions. Be that as it may, consultants often run into similar problem structures and indicators, given the parallels between companies and markets, which enable them to transfer methods or which provide input for improved or new methodological concepts.

These ideas are scrutinized, honed and refined in dialogue with colleagues and clients, and sometimes even through empirical studies – or they are rejected. In this way, practical consulting experience makes a contribution to the advancement of methods, which in turn helps improve consulting quality.

The leaders in the consulting industry therefore make targeted investments in building and expanding their knowledge base and encourage the transfer of knowledge. Some examples of this are:

- Intensive training of junior consultants
- Regular internal training seminars
- Support of postgraduate attainments such as MBA and doctoral degrees through limited, paid leaves of absence
- Round-the-clock access to intranet-based knowledge management systems
- Development of international practice groups for certain consulting fields
- Cultivation of external networks for dialogue with company mangers and scientists
- Initiation of issue-research projects to derive new knowledge

3.   The use of methods in strategy consulting

Strategic management consulting firms serve a demanding clientele. Their advice is sought both by industry leaders, who are not content to rest on their laurels and are ready to set themselves new goals, and by companies in critical situations, who are trying to get back on the road to success.

 Strategic management consulting helps clients to create clear competitive advantages and, thus, increase enterprise value over the long term. Operative improvements alone cannot bring about above-average achievement. Rather, fundamental changes are necessary, which take advantage of the growth and earnings potential of the company in a sustainable manner. This requires specially tailored, innovative solutions – not standard formulas. The consulting team and the top executives of the client company must be willing to call the conventional wisdom of the industry into question. This is less a matter of bringing forth lofty visions, than of adopting a non-biased perspective and approach based on the comprehensive analysis of objective figures, data and facts as opposed to subjective opinions or liberal ideas.

The companies are right to value the functionality of solutions above all else. The most wonderful, smoothly presented strategy is useless if it breaks down during implementation and fails because potential stumbling blocks were overlooked or underestimated – or if it fails due to the lack of specific instructions. Therefore, strategy projects must be designed to achieve results that are measurable and testable, and that provide clear direction and defined parameters for success. A survey of German companies with revenues greater than 100 million euros, conducted in 2003 by the market research institution TNS Emnid, concluded that this is the ideal shared by 90 percent of consulting clients.

The expertise of the consultant in matters of methodology is also called for in cooperation with clients for the selection of the relevant criteria for success. The benchmarks must not only reliably show the position of the company at the start of the project and how far it has come in the end, but must also be subject to influence by means of the measures applied and be easily and quickly calculable.

As a rule, two levels can be identified with regard to the use of methods in strategy consulting. Superior and sustained competitive advantage is best achieved by capitalizing on the combination of both strategic and operative potential (figure 1):

Strategic full potential means that the company aims to build up its market position (including entry into new markets, in which the company has previously held a zero market share). If this is accomplished, the company can not only achieve higher revenues, but also improve profit margins.

Operative full potential is concerned with the use of less complex structures, leaner processes and other measures to increase productivity and lower costs, so that the company can reach earnings targets appropriate to its market position.

Capitalising on Operative and Strategic Potential

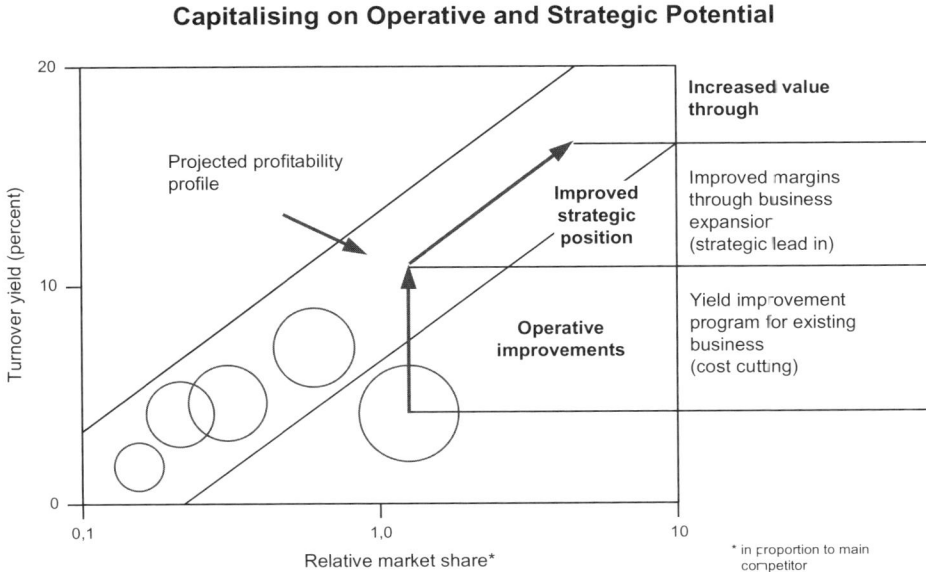

Fig. 1. Capitalising on operative and strategic potential

Accordingly, the management concepts used to diagnose the problem and to formulate and implement the solution can be categorized according to their character as either more strategic or operative in nature. In addition, there are also neutral, supportive instruments. An example of these is given below.

Since it is concerned with identifying the company's most attractive business areas and areas for expansion, the Portfolio Analysis method mentioned above is an example of a strategic analysis and valuation instrument.

Similarly, the Share of Wallet is primarily a strategic approach. That is to say, it is implemented to identify and make use of untapped sales potential in connection with existing clients. This is based on a calculation of a client's or client group's overall demand or procurement budget volumes in a specific needs category (wallet) and the portion of this that is being met by the assessing company (share of wallet). The Share of Wallet method, however, not only serves to rank clients (client groups) in terms of potential for expansion in order for the company to formulate an appropriate growth strategy. It also extends into the area of operative execution. For example, non-clients and clients are classified according to their revenue generating potential and the level of capitalization on this potential, in order to better target sales structures and thus, increase sales success and efficiency. The sales performance of individual clients can also be controlled through Share of Wallet analysis, both short and long term.

A related method complex, which is also geared toward capitalization on existing customer potential and is therefore strategic in character, is CRM. It is not short-term, computer-aided campaigns, often considered annoying by the recipients, that deliver lasting success. Rather, it is the right mix of product, supplementary, and information offers together with ongoing targeted communication with clients that make a winning combination. The strategic plan must be right on.

Conversely, instruments such as TQM (Total Quality Management), Business Process Re-engineering or Lean Management are counted as operative methods, because they serve to improve the company's earnings in relation to its market position. SCM (Supply Chain Management)is another example of this.

The prime directive of strategy also applies to the operative methods: Instruments that accord with the strategic plan hold the greatest promise of success. Doubts concerning the strategic course or isolated implementation imperil success. In strategic consulting, the operative methods play a key role, especially in putting the chosen strategy decisively into action. Ambitious goals cannot be achieved in any other way.

An example of a neutral instrument is benchmarking, whereby comparisons are made with the sector leader. This serves to expose strengths and weaknesses, thus contributing to the strategic or operative selection of a business location. It is, however, of no help in answering the question as to how a company can achieve the crucial and sustainable competitive advantages needed to take the lead itself – in particular with regard to issues of how to capitalize on potential.

4.   A system of coordinates for strategy development

The basis of all strategic planning is the question: Am I doing the right thing? Only after this fundamental question has been answered is the follow-up asked: How do I do it the right way? The methods discussed up to this point have primarily addressed the *how*, after the basic strategic option to be considered or implemented has been determined.

They offer little assistance, however, when it comes to the decision as to which strategic option is most suited in the given situation, taking into account ongoing developments, to clearly attain the desired competitive advantages and, thereby, achieve sustainable profitable growth. For instance, should the company grow organically or through M&A? Should it focus more sharply on increasing market coverage, i.e. new customer acquisition, or on improving capitalization on existing customer potential? These methods are equally unavailing as guideposts marking the right strategic course towards growth – in the sense of a pattern of defined steps to follow.

The challenge is to set up a system of strategic coordinates that offers management or the consulting team a basis for decision-making concerning the company's location and operations, and is therefore able to serve as a general procedural framework, providing room for organizational learning.

Such a strategic meta-method has been developed by Bain & Company based on a comparative long-term analysis of company data, in-depth case studies and practical consulting experience (Zook, Allen 2001). The goal of the empirical analysis was to determine the key strategic factors in the long-term success of a company. To this end, Bain examined the performance of more than 2,600 stock exchange listed companies from the late 1980's with annual revenues of over USD 500 million.

Out of this group, those companies were isolated that demonstrated profitable growth throughout the 10-year period under review. More specifically, companies that achieved:

- Average real annual growth (adjusted for inflation) of 5.5 percent for revenue and earnings respectively.
- Revenues outmatching capital costs, including share price increases and dividends.

Those solid, sustained value creators, who fulfilled all three criteria, were subsequently examined more closely.

The principal results of the study show that only about one in ten companies achieves sustainable profitable growth. Some 80 percent of these solid value creators attribute their success to a strong and well-defined core business. In these areas, they maintain a market leading position, which is more important than the attractiveness of the market itself. Companies that are successful over the long-term achieve growth through consistent capitalization on the core business and expansion in adjacent segments that serve to strengthen the core.

The challenge for management therefore lies in finding the answer to four key strategic questions:

- Which areas belong to the company's core business?
- How great is the total revenue and earnings potential of this core – and how can the company capitalize on it?
- Which adjacent segments can contribute toward strengthening and expanding the core?
- How much potential does the core business hold over the long-term?

In essence, the development and implementation of a core-oriented strategy entails focusing on those segments, in which the company can achieve the most competitive advantage based on its individual strengths, and working to maintain and build upon these strengths. This cannot be achieved through one massive effort. Rather, this strategic undertaking should be considered an ongoing process of change and learning.

The success of any strategic move by the company depends wholly upon the correct definition of its core business: If the boundaries of the core business are set too broadly, the company runs a danger of becoming disconcerted and perhaps financially over extended. If it is too narrowly defined, the company relinquishes opportunities for growth and earnings.

The definition of the core business is best achieved in three steps. First, five criteria are examined in order to narrow down the relevant market, i.e. the arena in which the company wishes to compete. These five areas are - clients, costs, (sales) channels, capabilities (e.g. technology, markets) and competitors. Then, an analysis is conducted based on these five C's to determine which areas are adjacent and can thus comprise a strategically valid unit. Finally, those segments are separated out which will allow the company to make best use of its strengths and in which it can accordingly achieve the greatest competitive advantage over the long term.

These segments constitute the core, for which a leading market position must be achieved or defended. The precondition for this is that the company recognizes the full potential of its core business and makes the fullest possible use of this potential, in order to stay a step ahead of prospective and existing competitors. The true potential of the core is often underestimated, leading companies to hastily shift focus to new areas, thus running danger of undermining the foundation of their business. Consequently, careful analysis is required if the company is to fully capitalize on the strategic and operative potential of the core. A Share of Wallet analysis, for example, can offer significant assistance in this case.

Further growth can be a achieved through expansion in adjacent segments (fig. 2). The selection of a segment for expansion is based on its proximity to the core, because the likelihood of success diminishes dramatically as expansion moves away from the core. A simple measure of distance has therefore been developed to reflect the level of connectivity between the core and new segments. Expansions at a medium distance from the core should be regarded with a particularly critical eye. Though, at first glance, they may appear to be closely related, such mid-distance expansions often hold unseen risks (Zook, Seidensticker 2004). Only after it is clear that a move into the targeted segment would serve to strengthen or complement the core, does it make sense to decide whether the company should build up the new business area itself or choose acquisition as the way forward.

Main Forms of Expansion

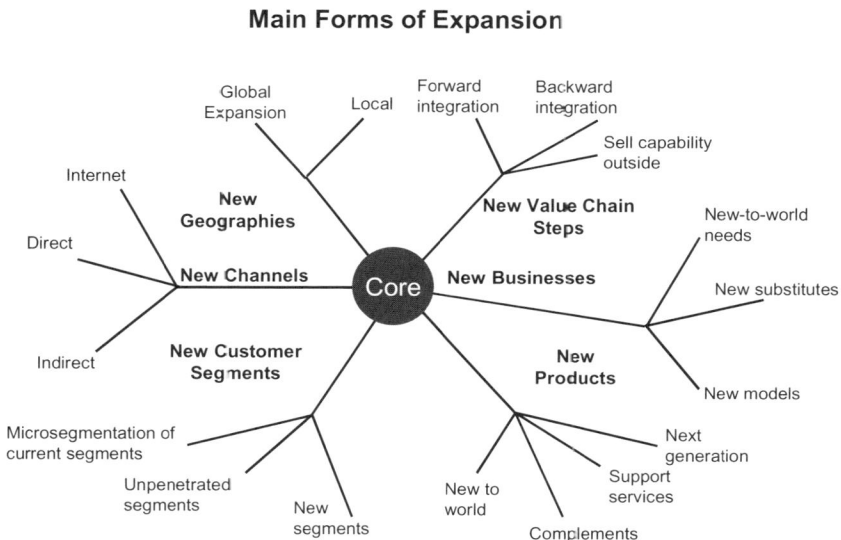

Fig. 2. Main forms of expansion

As beneficial as individual moves may seem, any expansion of the core increases the complexity of the company, thereby adding to the danger of the company overstretching itself. It is therefore advisable for companies to occasionally examine whether or not the expanded business portfolio maintains an adequately sharp focus, and to trim off non-strategic areas where necessary in order to strengthen growth and earnings power. Companies must also review, and possibly also reset the boundaries of the core if substantial changes occur in the market – e.g. through new technologies, revolutionary business models or government (de)regulation.

This brings the process full circle and a new strategy cycle can begin. In all cases, however, the aim is to competently use methods to take fact-based decisions and systematically implement solutions.

References

Fink, Dietmar (2004): Management Consulting 2004 – Trends und Kompetenzen in der Management-Beratung, Verlag Vahlen, Bonn.

Ming, Josef/Seikowsky, Fritz (2001): Strategische Unternehmensberatung im Internet-Zeitalter – Herausforderungen und Lösungsansätze, in: Siegwart, Hans/Mahari, Julan I. (eds.), Management Consulting, Verlag Vahlen, Munich.

Rigby, Darrell (2003): Management Tools 2003: An Executives Guide, Bain & Co, Boston.

Zook, Chris/Allen, James (2001): Erfolgsfaktor Kerngeschäft, Econ Verlag, Munich.

Zook, Chris/Seidensticker, Franz-Josef (2004): Die Wachstumsformel – Vom Kerngeschäft zu neuen Chancen, Carl Hanser Verlag, Munich.

Thought Leadership – In Action

Michael Träm

1. A.T. Kearney as example of an organisation striving for excellence

The term "Thought Leadership" reflects ambition and even illusion. However, it has recently become a buzzword used by many who want to ensure that everybody knows their thinking is top-notch and their output excellent. We would like to understand this term in the sense of its original meaning and bring it to life in our day-to-day consulting work.

A successful management consultancy provides a good example of how important thought leadership is and how much can be achieved if everyone in a company contributes to gaining and maintaining this thought leadership in as many fields as possible. Fresh and innovative thinking, deep knowledge and various skills linked together in teams and internal networks make an impact on the client organisations A.T. Kearney, one of the leading consultancies worldwide, supports. Only by applying first-rate thinking can a consultancy execute what today's clients expect: take an outsider's perspective, analyse critically, challenge existing concepts, come up with ideas, develop concepts and implement viable solutions worth the large amounts of money that companies spend on their consultants.

In fact, clients' expectations and our own standards are our guidelines. We base our work on what the clients need in their given situation, and we direct our thinking along the lines of current issues to achieve thought leadership – not in a remote mode, but in a down-to-earth and solution-oriented way. It is no coincidence that a client senior manager recently deemed A.T. Kearney "brilliantly practical." Other consultancies may have other attributes according to their specific focal points.

Brilliantly practical – this fantastic compliment translates what clients nowadays seek when hiring management consultants. From the client's perspective, consultants should do everything they can to bring their deep knowledge and expertise to bear on the client's situation. This expectation applies not only to specific circumstances, but also to the day-to-day business a company is engaged in, to the business dynamics, cost and margin drivers, and so on. Furthermore, consultants should be able to fully understand the implications of the current situation with respect to both the top and bottom line. So much for the "practical" aspect.

This practical view would not be very valuable without the "brilliance" which is a second asset that clients value in their consultants. Brilliance is what experienced and long-standing managers, who work in a line or staff position of an organisation, often tend to lose once they have acquired greater in-depth experience. Consultants who maintain the outside view, despite the long hours they spend in a client company, can more easily contribute brilliant thoughts that are best when they are practical, strategic and far-sighted at the same time.

In this context, a consulting firm, such as A.T. Kearney, relies on three assets – all of which are intangibles. These three assets include

- clients
- people
- intellectual capital

Only an ongoing interaction among these three assets constitutes *Thought Leadership*, which every consulting firm tries to establish in one way or another.

In light of the transition of the consulting industry, all consulting firms preparing for the future enhance and extend their high-level strategy offerings to include substantial topics such as innovation and pricing, the development of strategic IT-based offerings, the addition of portfolio restructuring to the cost reduction offerings – all of which are indispensable for their clients today. Thanks to their consultants, clients can achieve greater efficiency and effectiveness, even in times of generally poor economic results. These and other dynamics in the market make it more important for management consultants to focus clearly on the three basic assets mentioned above.

2.   Clients: Working *with* them – not *for* them

Let's start with the first asset - the clients who "come first" in all distinguished consultancies. Any professional service firm that does not have the means or the assets in terms of production sites, machines and the like in place builds on client relationships. Based on A.T. Kearney's experience, most of the satisfied clients come back to a reliable consulting partner whenever a problem arises. Because more than 70 percent of business is repeat business – this varies from consultancy to consultancy – a database with client data, in addition to knowledge about their organization and their individuality, is a priceless asset.

How can a consultancy ensure that they are the "consultants of choice", the consultants their clients prefer to work with? We see three main factors that constitute a good client relationship and we are confident this applies to most management consultancies: We listen to our clients, we build trust through intense collaboration, and we share knowledge and experience:

- **Listen to the client:**
  - It pays off in the very beginning, and repeatedly in the later stages of a relationship with a client organization, to listen carefully and actively to the issues and problems it currently faces. What does the CEO find important, what are his concerns, his priorities, his sine-qua-nons? How do his ideas fit with market reality? On the other hand, how do his managers and employees perceive the initiatives he has driven and the plans he has made? How do external stakeholders view the situation of the company from an outside

perspective? The entire organization commits more easily to the outcomes of a consulting project if all key members have been involved and heard.

- It also is important to show empathy or even sympathy with the client firm at critical junctions or turning points in corporate history. A consultant who goes for facts and nothing but the facts will do no more than deliver an expert report, which the client firm can choose to follow or not. If the consulting team interacts more closely and on a personal level with the entire management team and with key employees, the more likely it is that the client firm will take ownership of the project and be more inclined to buy into the recommendations made. In the long term, clients will live more easily with the consequences than they would if they had not been involved in the first place.

- All this is unthinkable without a consultant's clear commitment to the project and to the client. If a consultant understands the issues and their implications, he has a decision to make: Would he and the entire team be able to help this company in the given situation, or would the team be reluctant to take on this task and refrain from offering its support? If the decision is made to serve this company and solve the problem in question, this means commitment to the task and assuming responsibility for all its implications.

- **Build trust:** Trust is a prerequisite of any client relationship. It is built through the quality of project work, but also through a number of chances consultants have to take in the course of their work:

  - Teaming and partnership are basic principles of consulting work and, in addition, offer chances for establishing trustful relationships in the client organisation. Client teams, who have seen consultants putting themselves in their shoes, are more likely to trust the consultants and their recommendations.

  - Those who lead the consulting teams by definition – managers, principals and partners – establish very close contacts to the client's top management. If senior consultants give the right advice and prove excellent counsels of their client peers, they will soon be in a position where a CEO and/or his closest colleagues will rely on their suggestions and draw on them before making decisions. Very often, these coaching relationships develop into close business friendships and they may involve advice not only in business, but also in political and even personal matters.

  - If, after a consulting project, an organization is able to improve its competitive position, to grow its value or to increase its sales. it has obtained tangible results. Whether these results meet or exceed the client's expectations, trust in the consultant will reach a peak. If these tangible results continue to be repeated over the next few years because the concept proves solid and reliable, and if the concept renders an excellent return on consulting investment, then of course the trust in the consultants increases accordingly. In this way, good work provides a sound basis for trust.

- **Share knowledge and experience:** Clients are top managers of organizations that strive for growth and profitability – ideally for both at the same time. Of course, they are open to opportunities to improve their business, even beyond a consulting project. That is where the broad knowledge base of a consulting company comes in.
  - Providing clients with knowledge materials in the form of White Papers, books, and even presentations and articles is a favour consultants frequently do their clients to keep them up to date with first-rate knowledge and new insight. This knowledge can also be distributed, shared, and reinforced by writing joint articles to communicate the success of a project.
  - Knowledge and experience can also be passed on to the client in a more personal setting. Encounters of this nature are often highly effective ways of mediating expertise. Regular meetings with client top management – even when there are no ongoing projects – keep the client well-informed about the latest trends and refresh the relationship. This also includes challenging clients on their concepts and giving them the possibility to share their successes, e.g. by offering them the chance to take part in awards (such as the GEO award organized jointly by A.T. Kearney and Wirtschaftswoche) or by industry discussions at conferences.

The examples above should help clarify the meaning of the "clients first" approach. Clients should not only come first when a decision about work priorities has to be made, they should come first in the mindset of the entire consulting organisation. And, last but not least, clients should come first in the context of each project and be the centre of each consultant's attention. Excellent consultants do not work *for* their clients but *with* their clients. By assigning mixed client/consultant teams, a consultancy makes sure the client feels he comes first and is at the centre of the consulting efforts. This is a long-standing tradition in leading management consultancies – long before customer relationship management (CRM) became an issue in other industries.

3. People: Develop consultants individually

"People matter" – this applies in particular to the consulting industry. If not backed by their consultants, clients would find it hard to get the support they really need in critical situations. Typically, the lack of resources, skills, knowledge or the lack of all of these makes it a real challenge for clients to manage important projects without external advisors. External consultants need broader knowledge, have to analyse more thoroughly, judge more critically and communicate more openly than most in-house resources would. Consultants are carefully selected and trained to a very high level in order to be able to provide excellent services.

The Importance of People

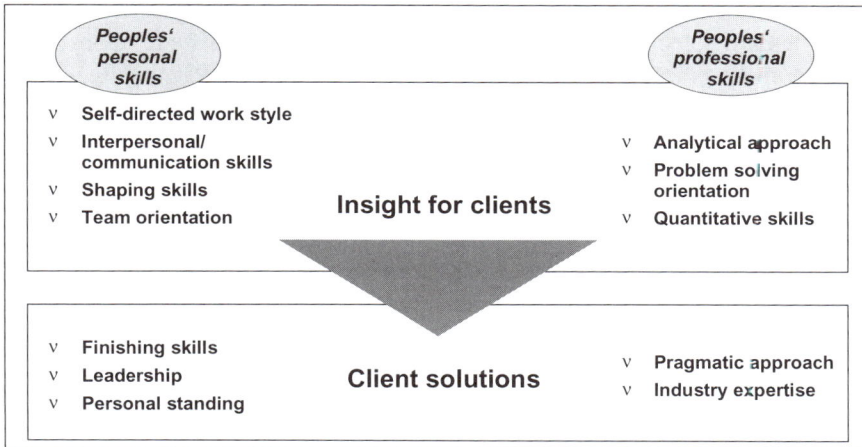

Fig. 1. People are the most important asset of any consultancy

As figure 1 shows, personal skills that can hardly be improved have to be complemented by professional skills that are upgraded on a continuous basis by every world-class consultancy. This may sound easy, it is, however, a hard and very cost-intensive task to develop people, to shape their career and to find the right place for each talent. Even recruitment is a very delicate matter and, unfortunately, it is not becoming easier. Personal development of a young consultant has to be tailored to the specific skill base of the person concerned. It also has to take into account the needs of the market in general and of specific industry issues. At the end of this bumpy road, both the company and the consultant need to decide whether it is best for him or her to stay with the firm and move up into leadership ranks, or to leave the consulting world and look for an attractive management position in an industry where all the acquired skills are needed and valued.

- **A fair chance for success**: As new consultants, young talents from various backgrounds are carefully selected based on the outstanding performance demonstrated in several rounds of recruiting. But this is only one side of the coin. On the other side the recruiting process clarifies matters for the potential new hire: Is this the right industry? Are these the right people to work with, can they perform the tasks and solve the problems they are facing? Are they aware of the downsides of consulting with extensive travel and little time for a private life? Does this career path satisfy their ambitions? People who are not only selected, but who wholeheartedly make a decision in favour of a consulting career, will quickly experience the upsides of consulting once they join the industry. The on-boarding process comprises international trainings, orientation days in the home office, getting to know mentors and, rapidly, more hands-on orientation – this time on the project they are assigned to.

- **Focus on personal development**: Needless to say, each individual stays an individual after joining a consultancy. No two people are alike. Therefore, no two people will develop in the same way. This is why at A.T. Kearney, for example, each development plan is compiled individually and the respective trainings are selected on the basis of the specific needs of each consultant. The development is tracked in annual evaluation processes. Regular feedback from a mentor ensures that consultants are aware of their "to dos" and that they get the support they need to work on their further development.
- **Two options for the future**: Once consultants have made a career in the consultancy of their choice, the moment may come when other professional challenges seem more interesting or their social life becomes more important. In this case, the consultants can be sure that the years spent in consulting will have shaped their personality and will have contributed to their overall knowledge base, so that many organisations will be interested in hiring them. The other possibility for consistently successful consultants is to move further up in their own firm and join the leadership team. In the first case, the reputable name and the network of the consultancy will enable a smooth transition and a good start at a traditional company. In the latter case, the senior consultant will become a leader who knows the company from all angles and is familiar with the strengths and weaknesses of the business.

The fact that consultants are "pampered" in a way not many companies would offer their new hires, has to do with the shortage of skilled people and with the demands of the job. When consulting firms, such as A.T. Kearney in Central Europe, make it among the top forty of the most popular employers in their country, this means that the good "balance between work and private life" has become a reality, forming a solid basis for a firm of thought leaders.

4. Intellectual capital: Share knowledge

Most of the knowledge within an organisation resides with and is related to the people who work for it. These people have built up expertise in their academic education, in previous jobs, in trainings, and on their projects. Together they constitute the collective knowledge of the consultancy. If a consultant leaves, a fair share of the knowledge goes with that person. Therefore, consulting companies who mostly act on the maxim of "up or out" or "grow or go" have to make sure that at least part of the critical knowledge is saved electronically as far as possible and can be accessed by everyone in the company.

Thought leadership is based on a good knowledge management and on the willingness of each individual to share knowledge and insights with others in the team and in the entire company. In this context it is important that a management consultancy has more than just electronic systems in place. A consultancy lives from a knowledge culture.

- **Know what we know**: Today, it is easy to record new methods and approaches developed on projects in the form of handbooks and case examples. Project debriefings and internal projects both form the basis of these files.
- **Extend knowledge and insights**: As intellectual capital is the quintessence of thought leadership, building knowledge on a regular basis is crucial for a consulting firm, which strives to stay one step ahead of clients in as many fields of knowledge as possible. This includes practical experience as well as intensive reading and reviewing the latest academic literature, market studies and research.
- **Make the most of it**: As long as the intellectual capital is not actively used and disseminated, it will not contribute to the competence and the brand of a consulting firm, thus failing to attract clients. If the material is not "lived", thought leadership is not recognised. Consultants should always speak openly and to a wide audience, write articles, make contributions to books and lecture at conferences. In addition, they should do it in a timely fashion, on the same day they come up with results. If they do not, the knowledge accumulated so far will be lost before anyone can benefit from their valuable insights and concepts.

A consulting firm striving for thought leadership by satisfying clients far beyond their basic demands should find the right balance between the three assets that such a firm relies on. There may be incremental differences by firm, but the opportunity to develop around clients, people, and intellectual capital is invaluable.

PART II

MANAGING CONSULTING FIRMS

The Challenge of Growth – How to Manage a Consultancy

Burkhard Schwenker

1. Introduction

Far-reaching changes in the business world are currently confronting corporate management with a number of major challenges. Just think of the way globalisation is affecting every industry, the way the use of electronic communications is making markets more transparent and the way new business models are taking shape. Whether these changes give rise to opportunities or risks depends on the quality of the management in each company. International strategy consultancies face the same challenges. They need to provide excellent advice on these issues to their clients and they must prove themselves in an environment of constant change. Their managers must likewise rise to the challenges ahead.

It is nevertheless important to take account of certain characteristics that distinguish consultancies from other companies (e.g. industrial firms) and that therefore impact their management. On the one hand, these include what can be termed "historical" characteristics, such as the use of knowledge as their key production factor and the preference given to partnerships as an organisational form. On the other hand, they include new industry-specific challenges, such as changed client expectations (clients now have experience with consultants) and the simple fact that the consulting market as a whole is singularly dynamic. In particular, consultancies need managers who can create a suitable organisational and personnel framework to accommodate the rapid growth that virtually all firms in this industry have experienced over the past twenty years.

So what exactly should the management of a strategy consultancy be like? How does it differ from the management of any other company? These are the questions that this paper seeks to answer. We will begin by outlining the aspects that are peculiar to management consultancies. Then we will discuss what these specifics mean, how they should be managed and how management consultancies can rise to the challenge of growth. Finally, we will examine current developments in the consulting sector – and the solutions that consultancies are finding to cope with them.

2.   The specifics of consultancies

For their clients, management consultancies act as innovation generators, optimisers, initiators – the catalysts of change, if you like. They help their clients to identify and analyse both problems and opportunities, and they formulate strategies to solve the problems and exploit the opportunities. As external, professional advisers called in for a limited period of time, they ensure that their clients are able to develop and tap their potential to the full. And these clients know exactly what results they expect to see from consulting projects: they want solutions that go beyond the concepts they are already using, but that still give due consideration to their individual situation.

In macro-economic terms, the existence of management consultancies is the result of increasing specialisation. Management consultancies handle tasks that arise only once or at irregular intervals. In so doing, they save their clients the trouble of having to maintain the corresponding capacity on a permanent basis. Since consultants perform these tasks for many companies in parallel, they accumulate a wealth of information about different industries, technologies and countries. They also develop special skills in analytical and problem-solving techniques. In addition to this experience and the resultant "economies of scale", clients benefit from the fact that external consultants can approach assignments with an objective, open mind. Consultancies thus give their clients an independent, outside view that is free from the constraints of day-to-day business, a perspective that removes the organisational blinkers.

Four main characteristics distinguish (large) strategy consultancies:

- they offer their services internationally on a project basis, i.e. they work for a limited period of time on specific issues for clients around the globe,
- they are knowledge companies whose very nature is to effect paradigm shifts by trading knowledge as a competitive advantage,
- independence and neutrality are fundamental to their sustained market success,
- they are organised as partnerships, i.e. they have no external shareholders.

These characteristics are explained below.

1. Large strategy consultancies work on hundreds of projects per year, projects that may also have a broad geographical spread. Management's job is to ensure appropriate staffing and quality worldwide. That in itself is a challenge, because consultancies have international workforces. Their individual country offices employ a mix of local consultants and support staff plus employees from other countries. Country specialists from the local or regional offices work on projects alongside functional or industry specialists from other countries. International project business places heavy demands on consultants. They have to be ready for deployment anywhere in the world, deliver consistent performance for a variety of clients in widely differing (corporate) cultures and form effective teams with other consultants and client staff. At the same time they must produce a constant stream of innovative but workable solutions that they implement in collaboration with their clients. Their own roots often mean

that teams of consultants represent all kinds of different cultural and educational backgrounds. Accommodating these factors at management level is of paramount importance in consultancies.

2. Knowledge is the core content of any consulting mandate. Clients buy in knowledge that they do not have internally, but that they need in order to add value. The sources from which consultancies draw their knowledge are many and varied (figure 1). For example, they include detailed knowledge of narrowly defined disciplines (legal aspects, technologies, statistical methods, occupational psychology, to name but a few), the consultancy's own empirical studies, analysis of research results delivered by academic institutions that collaborate with consultancies, or publications supplied by commercial information providers (market research firms, intelligence providers, trade journals, etc.). The specific knowledge available to individual companies naturally also encompasses the experience they have gained from past projects. This is the basis on which they earn a reputation as specialists in certain areas or industries. The diverse educational backgrounds of the consultants themselves ensure broad coverage of a wide range of knowledge fields. That is why management consultancies employ a colourful mix of economists, legal experts, engineers, scientists and people with a background in the humanities. Knowledge is critical to the success of consultancies. To make optimum use of this resource, they must therefore embed it on three levels. Firstly, a uniform enterprise-wide technological platform must exist on which information can be entered, edited and retrieved. Secondly, standardised processes must be defined to govern the way knowledge is shared or fed into the system. Forums – thematic forums on the intranet, for instance – must also be created to encourage the pooling of information. Thirdly and most importantly, sharing information must be a natural part of everyday work. Such a culture can, for example, be encouraged by making knowledge-sharing incentives an integral feature of employee appraisals.

Consultancies as Knowledge Catalysts

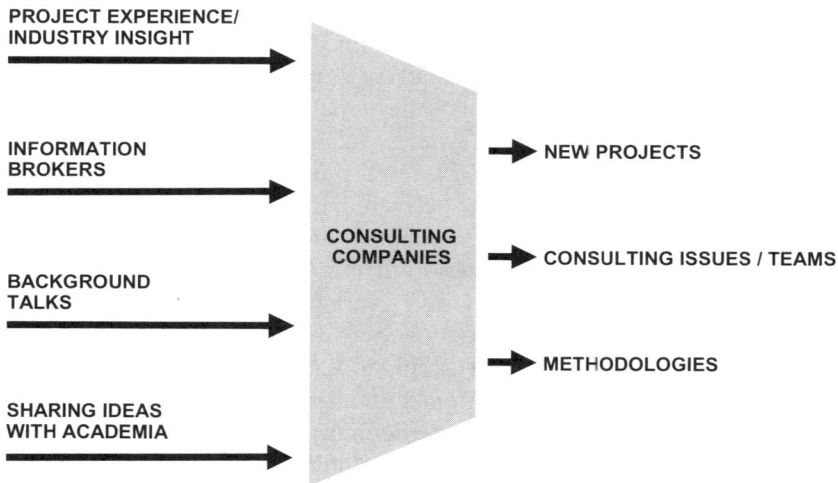

PROJECT EXPERIENCE/
INDUSTRY INSIGHT

INFORMATION
BROKERS

CONSULTING
COMPANIES

NEW PROJECTS

BACKGROUND
TALKS

CONSULTING ISSUES / TEAMS

METHODOLOGIES

SHARING IDEAS
WITH ACADEMIA

Fig. 1. As knowledge catalysts consultancies are mediators and enablers of progress

Management consultancies apply their knowledge in two ways. Firstly, before and during concrete projects they use it to satisfy the considerable demand for knowledge about the client company's market environment, industry trends and competitors. During collaboration with the client, information from the client company itself receives the most attention. Secondly, they use their knowledge to develop new issues and refine existing concepts and methods. Ultimately, project work also benefits, because the knowledge gained here ensures that each client's assignments are resolved using state-of-the-art resources. In other words, innovation gives the consultant's client a competitive edge.

3 Another characteristic feature of consulting firms is their obligation to remain strictly unbiased and independent. The management must implement and ensure compliance with a code of conduct that effectively makes consultants immune to all attempts by third parties to sway them. The results of consulting projects must be founded solely and solidly on objective analysis. That is the only way for consultancies to maintain their good reputation, which is crucial to their market (and fee) position. If consultancies violate these standards, they are not "only" in breach of contract, it would also do irreparable damage to their reputation. Accordingly, the inside details of projects must be treated in the strictest confidence. Moreover, any conflicts of interest that arise in the course of a project must always be resolved internally. "Chinese walls" between project teams working on assignments for rival clients safeguard confidentiality and autonomy in such cases. These requirements have also been formalised in the codes of

conduct published by consulting associations. The details are fleshed out in individual project and work contracts.

4. Finally, partnerships are the organisational form of choice for strategy consultancies. There are several reasons for this. One is that to be a partner – an active owner – means to assume direct, personal responsibility for the company. Since they participate in profits and value growth, partners feel the impact of the company's success (or failure) on their own income. Partners therefore naturally identify more strongly with the company and are more motivated to guide it to success than is the case with executive employees. A further benefit of the partnership model is that the owners are involved in pivotal corporate decisions, such as strategic investments in new areas of competence, geographic expansion and the choice of new partners and appointment of managers. As a result, these decisions enjoy broad-based legitimacy. This in turn makes it easier for those whose opinions occasionally differ from those of the majority to remain committed. Obviously, the number of decisions made by all partners must be kept to a bare minimum if a partnership is to work efficiently. All other decisions affecting the company as a whole should be entrusted to corporate management.

These benefits for partners also create a tremendous incentive for all employees to want to become partners. It increases their motivation to produce excellent work and thereby build a fulfilling career for themselves. Last, but not least, the prospect of becoming part owner of a successful consultancy is also attractive to potential recruits.

These four characteristics stake out the broad lines for the management of a consultancy to keep the company on track for success. The extraordinary growth that the consulting market has experienced in the past adds a special challenge. In the decade from 1990 to 2000, the global volume of this market rocketed from 25 billion euros to 114 billion euros (figure 2). The latter half of the 1990s brought annual growth rates of 17.5%. In 2002 the consulting market decreased, while in 2003 the market is expected to level off at 119 billion euros. There are, however, clear reasons why the demand for consulting services should pick up again in the years ahead. These reasons largely reflect the requirements being placed on client companies, whose demand for greater efficiency and growth strategies is substantial as markets continue to change rapidly. After a short "breather", the trend towards mergers will revive as there is still plenty of potential for market consolidation and, hence, for further economies of scale and synergies. Finally, the deployment of new information technologies has anything but peaked. Firms that want to optimise the way they plan and implement the organisational changes that ensue – the outsourcing of non-core activities, closer networking with value-adding partners and the creation of virtual structures – will in future continue to rely on the expertise of consultancies. Furthermore, the macro-economic division of labour between consultants and other companies that we mentioned earlier will also drive fresh market growth. Consultancies' specialisation as temporary external service providers gives them a competitive edge.

Market Volume Growth – World 1990-2003 [EUR bn]

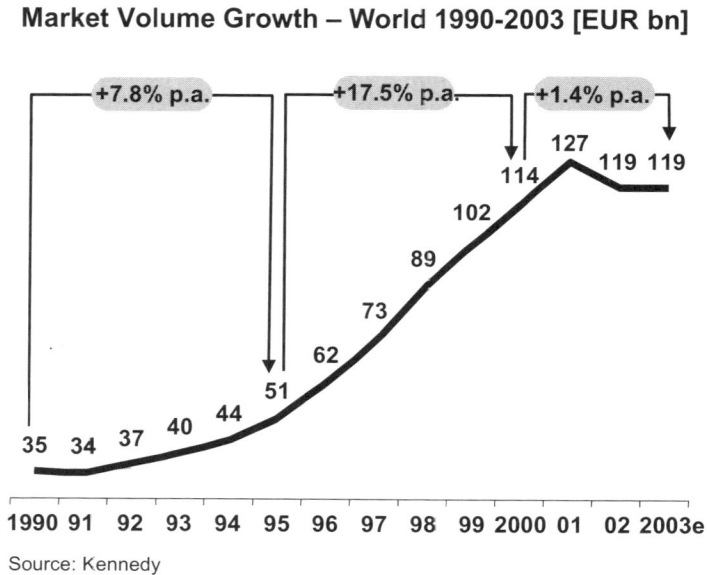

Source: Kennedy

Fig. 2. The consulting market was very dynamic in the 1990s

Strong market growth is not the only factor that is obliging consultancies to grow, it is merely the most obvious. Any company that grows more slowly than the market implicitly loses market share. Since their key goals – global presence, superior quality, the ability to innovate and the chance to offer employees excellent career opportunities – are intimately linked to growth, consultancies also have a natural compulsion to expand.

Let us look first at global presence. All large management consultancies have to operate a worldwide network of offices. They need to be on the ground in Europe, America and Asia, the key business centres, but also in emerging markets. The globalisation of consultancies began in the 1960s and went hand in hand with the increasing internationalisation of large corporations. True to the motto "follow the client", the consultancies sought to help their clients to penetrate new markets. This allowed them to nurture closer client relationships and, at the same time, to acquire new clients in different countries. However, maintaining a global presence also means being able to offer uniform quality standards, consistent methodologies and identical content. Such a presence can only be realised if a company achieves critical mass, not just at its home base but also in the different international markets. The only way to do this is to grow strongly and continually. Another consideration is that internationalisation is imperative if a consultancy is to sustain strong growth when its domestic market becomes saturated.

Like globalisation, there is also a dual correlation between the objectives of quality and growth: the two take it in turns at being cause and effect. On the one hand, the quality of consulting work is the principal lever that secures lasting client loyalty, acquires new clients and consolidates a consultancy's competitive position. Since consulting is based on experience, a consultancy's reputation is only ever as good as its most recent project. A single failure can detract from and, at times, even destroy a company's standing. On the other hand, growth is needed to generate free cash flow. Cash flow in turn allows companies to invest in better processes and methods, in a broader knowledge base and in recruiting and developing staff. All of which helps to maintain a high level of quality. Growth is thus not merely an effect but also a cause of quality.

By developing new concepts, consultancies have contributed significantly to advancing the discipline of business administration. Management techniques such as scientific management and shareholder value management originate from consultancies, as do new organisational concepts and innovative methods of analysis. The ability to develop such concepts and translate them into practice thus becomes the hallmark of every consultancy. Here again, the relationship with growth is reciprocal: only those companies that invest relentlessly can safeguard their innovative capabilities. To do so, they must invest in:

- systems that allow knowledge to be tapped, projects to be managed and products to be developed,
- maintaining external networks, through contact with universities and academic institutions,
- developing human resources by means of MBA and PhD programs as well as internal and external seminars.

Conversely, this investment is possible only if the company's growth generates sufficient cash flow. Then again, the ability to innovate is itself a condition of growth, in that it combines with operational performance to determine the reputation and competitive position of a consultancy. Clients expect their consultants to develop and implement creative strategies. Standard solutions give them no competitive edge and therefore add no value.

Lastly, consultancies must grow if they want to offer their staff attractive career prospects (figure 3). International assignment, projects in different industries and with varying functional content, wide-ranging development opportunities, compensation commensurate with performance and upward mobility to the level of co-ownership are conditions that attract highly talented applicants and motivate employees to deliver outstanding performance. Again, this performance fuels growth, and this growth ensures that there is enough money to pay for the "benefits" described – and that there are enough top positions for high performers to fill.

The Importance of Growth for Consulting Firms

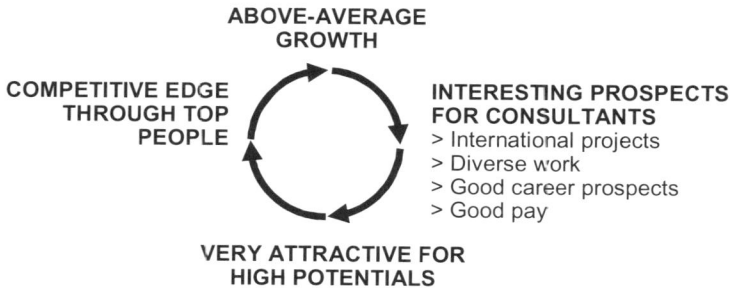

ABOVE-AVERAGE
GROWTH

COMPETITIVE EDGE
THROUGH TOP
PEOPLE

INTERESTING PROSPECTS
FOR CONSULTANTS
> International projects
> Diverse work
> Good career prospects
> Good pay

VERY ATTRACTIVE FOR
HIGH POTENTIALS

Fig. 3. Consultancies must grow to offer their people good prospects

The bottom line is that consultancies can only achieve their goals if they grow. Since growth is indispensable to every consultancy, managing growth naturally becomes a core task of corporate management. Before moving on to look in detail at the requirements placed on management in the section that follows, the discussion so far already allows us to identify a number of objectives that those who lead consultancies must pursue to keep their companies on track for growth. They must aim to:

- select and quickly recruit the most talented applicants,
- integrate new staff in the organisation and, in particular, in the consultancy's culture,
- provide ongoing training to encourage continuous employee development,
- make provision for systematic key account management,
- create the conditions for permanent innovation and product development,
- make quality the key yardstick by which every product is measured,
- enhance the company's reputation by delivering excellent project results, cultivating the brand and producing valuable publications.

3. How to manage a consultancy – and its growth

The previous section described the features that distinguish consultancies from other companies. We now need to examine what really matters when it comes to managing a consultancy, i.e. what the crucial success factors are.

To clearly understand these success factors, we must first briefly discuss a number of issues that are important in the context of consultancy management:

- management is never performed as an exclusive function, divorced from or independent of operational business. In all consultancies, managers on every level (both decentralised and corporate management) always remain responsible for certain operational duties. In other words, they continue to acquire clients and manage projects. To a certain extent, managers always stay actively involved on the "shop floor".

- management positions at consulting firms are usually filled at relatively short notice, i.e. there is no standard development path that leads there. Managers at industrial companies slowly grow into their executive positions, while managers at consultancies take on heavy responsibility all at once when they become partners. This abrupt change is at best mitigated by the fact that project managers exercise limited management functions in some areas.

- managing a consultancy is complex in that it is very much a people business. Marked cultural differences exist within individual teams. The industry as a whole features many strong personalities (and not a few *prima donnas!*). Finally, the way teams think and act varies considerably depending on the industry they serve. The consulting industry is, in other words, heterogeneous by nature.

Management must respond to these issues – all the more so given the fast-paced nature of the consulting business. If it does this, it will discover the need to focus on five key aspects:

- clear responsibilities
- quality assurance
- systems
- internal services
- corporate culture

The section below discusses each of these aspects in detail.

3.1 Clear responsibilities

The structure of a consultancy comprises several levels that exist in parallel and usually interact because the market demands it (figure 4). Each of these levels assumes different responsibilities:

- competence centres (CCs) or "practices" bundle content-specific or thematic knowledge and skills
- regional units and country organisations are in charge of the consulting offices
- key account management is responsible for looking after major clients

Business Dimensions of a Consultancy

COMPANY

Competence areas   Regions, countries   Key accounts

OFFICES

Task for the company's executive team: Simultaneous managing of the different business dimensions

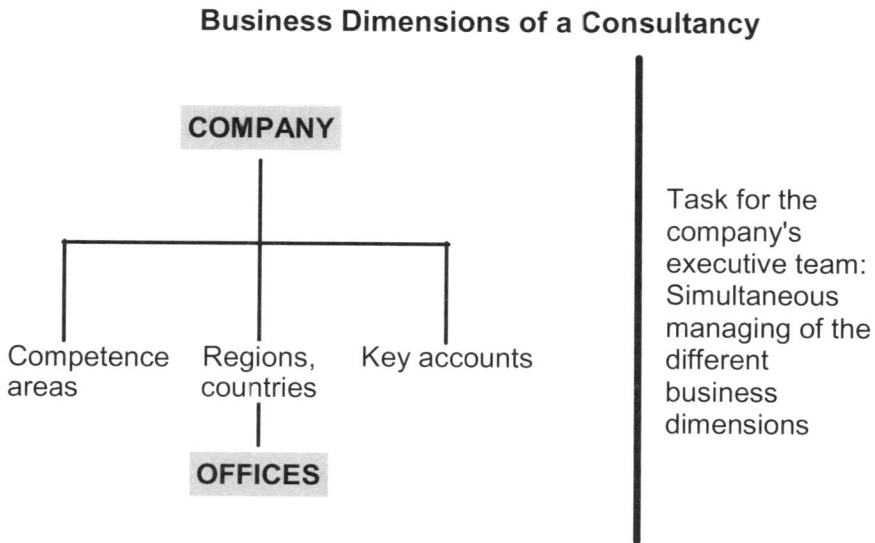

Fig. 4. Managing a consultancy is complex because of its different business dimensions

The people who manage the competence centres are responsible for handling CC-specific projects. They ensure that functional and industry-specific expertise is continually expanded. They are also responsible for the market and delivery performance of the individual CCs. To make optimum use of functional and industry-specific competence, most consultancies organise their competence centres in a matrix structure. For this reason, mixed teams that combine functional and industry-specific experts work together on certain projects. Besides ensuring a broad base of relevant skills, this approach also makes teams flexible enough to accommodate any changes to the focus of a project. It also fosters close relationships with clients and the ability to generate synergies between different areas of functional and industry-specific expertise. The management of the CCs concerned is responsible for coordinating collaboration between the different CCs.

Countries or regions in which a consultancy has an extensive presence are also usually organised as CCs. In such cases, the CCs in individual countries form subsets of the corresponding international, enterprise-wide CCs. However, new or smaller countries or regions often do not have the critical size for such fine organisational distinctions. This is where it makes sense to follow the structure of existing key accounts. When this happens, the industry-specific focus of key accounts determines which CCs are set up as soon as the business has grown to sufficient size. There seem to be hardly any consultancies that operate all elements of their matrix structure in every country. Instead, they import the necessary expertise from larger offices in line with project requirements.

Key accounts are important not only as a way of organising the business of consultancies in different countries. The most important key accounts should be attached to corporate HQ. This places the responsibility for these accounts in the hands of top management. Ideally, one key account should be entrusted to one partner to ensure that major clients always have a clearly identifiable point of contact. Where clients focus clearly on one industry and operate in countries where a consultancy maintains CCs, it can also make sense to define key accounts at the level of the CC.

It is up to corporate management to ensure that these different levels can interact smoothly. To do so, they must first define the relationships that are to exist between them. That means specifying not only the structure, but also the procedures that the various levels should adopt in dealing with each other. All consultancies have found it expedient not to define such processes in detail but to create a broad framework that allows the organisational units sufficient flexibility. Moreover, neither structures nor processes can ever be carved in stone. They must be adapted whenever they no longer optimally help the company to realise its goals, or when changed conditions necessitate adjustments.

Precisely for the previously described reason that consultancies have a multidimensional structure, it is imperative for the management on every level – including top management – to have clearly defined responsibilities. The management of each organisational unit must be clearly assigned to one specific partner, or to a specific body consisting of several partners. The same applies to related tasks such as target definition and budget compliance monitoring. Why is this so important? Because wherever multidimensional organisations exist, there is always the danger that reporting lines may be duplicated or become blurred. In the interests of efficient organisation, such a situation should always be avoided. If responsibility is to be discharged properly, management needs to have the right metrics to measure compliance with fee volume targets, for instance, or to monitor sales and earnings. It is also important to measure a unit's contribution to the company's further development in areas such as issue development and brand profiling. Such metrics give top management a tool that helps them to measure the performance of CC, country and key account managers. The company's overall progress can be monitored on the same basis. In addition, top management has a solid basis on which to take action if there is any threat to target compliance. Where necessary, it can also adapt metrics to reflect changed conditions. Incidentally, clearly defined responsibilities are crucial not only to the success of individual projects. They are equally critical in ensuring that internal processes in departments such as Research, Human Resources, Controlling and IT all operate smoothly. The people responsible for these departments should therefore report to members of the top management team.

3.2 Quality assurance

The assignment and fulfilment of responsibilities is closely linked to the need to safeguard quality, as discussed in the previous section. How can management assure the quality of the services the company offers? Three issues are of relevance here:

The first concerns selecting and developing personnel – the most important asset – in a way that enables high-quality performance to be delivered. Personnel selection is a key management task, as is personnel development. This applies all the more to the practice of assigning people to projects in a way that promotes their personal and professional development. This can, for example, be done by varying the content of projects or assigning people to projects in different industries. Consultancies have set up mentoring systems in all these areas. These systems are designed to ensure that a fair balance is struck between the interests of the company and those of the individual consultant.

At the same time, the management must prescribe clear quality targets that can be measured by indicators such as customer satisfaction, the number of follow-up orders or the contribution made to the company's development. It is the job of top management to define these quality targets. Measurement should then take place on different levels (figure 5): How did the individual consultant perform? And what about the project team? The competence centre? The country? And so on. The important thing is to measure quality regularly and to define quality on the basis of an internal benchmarking system.

Performance Indicators in Consulting

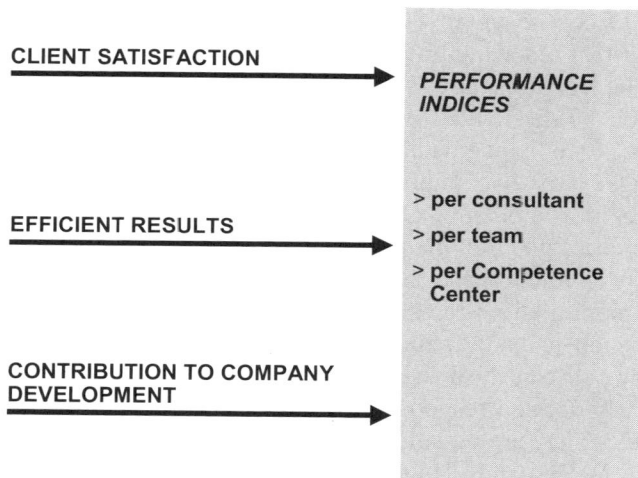

CLIENT SATISFACTION

PERFORMANCE INDICES

> per consultant

EFFICIENT RESULTS

> per team

> per Competence Center

CONTRIBUTION TO COMPANY DEVELOPMENT

Fig. 5. Open internal benchmarking in particular achieves transparency regarding performance quality

Management must give high-quality execution top priority. Quality assurance too must be acknowledged internally as a valid management principle. An appropriate culture must exist if these goals are to be achieved. In this whole process, top management plays a decisive role not only because it defines the quality targets. It must also formulate corporate principles and live them out for the rest of the company to see. One way in which it can do this is by actively monitoring the quality assurance process and regularly reporting on current quality levels. On a project level, the aim must be to maximise transparency and talk openly about any mistakes that are made. It is no secret that this is easier said than done. True, consultancies are known for being open and direct in what they say. However, this principle must be demonstrated over and over again, day in, day out. It is also important to remember that openness is not an end in itself. It only becomes truly valuable if the overriding objective, when conflicts arise, is to work together to find the best possible solution. Merely pointing out mistakes has never helped anyone to make progress. This is where managerial staff are called on to show where improvement is possible in each individual situation.

3.3 Systems

Consultancies need a series of systems that all interact smoothly if they are to meet their business objectives. The term "systems" is used here to mean tools that speed up the process flow within a consultancy. Key components of such systems are fundamental IT (e.g. databases and query systems), stored content (e.g. consultant profiles and information about competitors) and rules that govern usage. The latter can, for example, determine which documents are stored where on the system. Two types of systems are of special importance:

- first, systems that relate directly to project execution – to the practice of adding value by providing consulting services. These systems support the entire project lifecycle, starting with the acquisition phase, focusing on actual project work and ending with post-completion and follow-up processes. The latter phase ensures that lessons learned and knowledge gained from the project are incorporated into future consulting activities.
- second, fast management information systems that keep internal management up to date on the latest developments at the company. Especially in an industry that devotes so much of its time and energy to project business, it is imperative to have a controlling tool that meets the highest possible standards on this score.

Top management must put in place the necessary systems and infrastructures to ensure fast access to high-quality information. Consultancies that know how to integrate these two types of system have a definite advantage. Every item of data they enter effectively becomes valuable information.

Consultancies have become the global leaders in the deployment of knowledge and human resources management systems. The nature of their business forced them to invest early on in designing the technology and content of these systems. Such investment enabled them to stand up to fierce pressure to innovate – and to organise their internal processes more efficiently. A disproportionate number of the case studies that today deal with these two issues are based on examples from the consulting community – a clear reflection of consultancy managers' early sensitivity to such issues. This sensitivity in turn allowed them to channel resources into forward-looking investments.

3.4 Internal services

Management must naturally look after the running of the company's consulting processes. But it must also commit to ensuring that adequate internal services are provided. There are three relevant types of services (figure 6): professional services that deliver direct input to the consulting teams (e.g. research and analysis, knowledge management, translation, editing and so on), process-related services (i.e. IT infrastructures, graphic design services, etc.) and significant support services such as human resources management and administrative services.

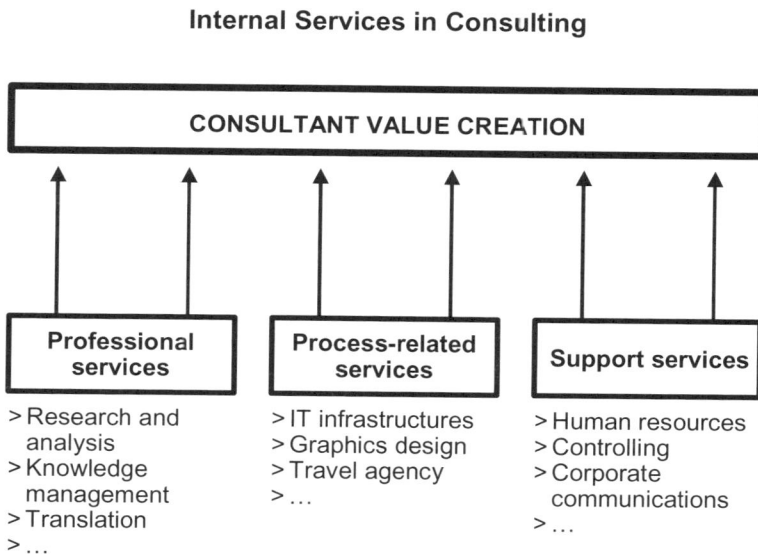

Internal Services in Consulting

CONSULTANT VALUE CREATION		
Professional services	**Process-related services**	**Support services**
> Research and analysis > Knowledge management > Translation > ...	> IT infrastructures > Graphics design > Travel agency > ...	> Human resources > Controlling > Corporate communications > ...

Fig. 6. Three types of internal services support consultant value creation

Different consultancies organise professional services in particular in a wide variety of ways. Some of these structures are simply a response to historical lines of internal development. Others reflect varying forms of consulting work. The tasks of business analysts, for instance, can either be pooled and executed at corporate level or delegated to individual project teams. Similarly, knowledge management can be a corporate function, or responsibility and execution can be devolved to decentralised units.

Regular reviews are an important part of internal service management: Are services in their current form still efficient? Do new forms of process or organisation now exist that could improve productivity? Consultancies in particular must be seen to "walk the talk" and apply the same benchmarking methods to themselves that they use with their clients. This helps them to cut costs and improve quality.

Service staff assigned to these three groups make up around one third of a consultancy's workforce. This is a sizeable cost block, and one that must be financed by the acquisition performance and productivity of the consultants. In the light of this fact, it is important for internal services to adhere to (and be measured by) the same performance-related principles as the consultants themselves. Here again, management must take the initiative. The usual answer is to evaluate internal service staff based on the same categories and processes that are used to appraise the consultants. Incidentally, this approach is the best way to encourage both sides to develop the same entrepreneurial mindset. As such, it actively prevents the emergence of two "parallel cultures" in one and the same company.

3.5 Corporate culture

Managing means establishing organisational hierarchies and processes and defining and sustaining information and communication processes. The corporate culture lays the foundation on which different parts of the company interlock as they should (figure 7). For consultancies, probably the ideal goal is to realise a performance-oriented culture of trust (which must then, of course, be lived out). Several things are needed to nurture such a culture.

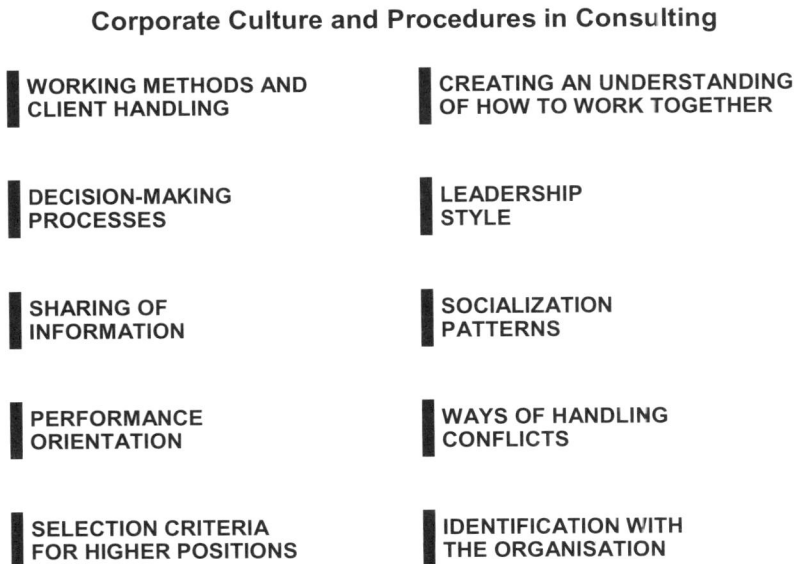

Corporate Culture and Procedures in Consulting

WORKING METHODS AND
CLIENT HANDLING

CREATING AN UNDERSTANDING
OF HOW TO WORK TOGETHER

DECISION-MAKING
PROCESSES

LEADERSHIP
STYLE

SHARING OF
INFORMATION

SOCIALIZATION
PATTERNS

PERFORMANCE
ORIENTATION

WAYS OF HANDLING
CONFLICTS

SELECTION CRITERIA
FOR HIGHER POSITIONS

IDENTIFICATION WITH
THE ORGANISATION

Fig. 7. Corporate culture should create a basis for many types of procedures

Firstly, a performance-oriented culture demands fast decision-making processes. These in turn necessitate a commitment to finding pragmatic solutions. And this commitment entails an attitude that is willing to accept decisions even when they go against one's own personal opinion. Another aspect is that decision processes must be made as transparent as possible. This makes it easier to give direction to the people affected by decisions, or to integrate them in making those decisions. It also makes it easier for people to understand the impact of decisions.

In addition, a consultancy must build on a shared understanding of performance orientation. It is the performance of each project team as a whole – and ultimately of the entire company – that matters most. There should be no rewards for individuals who massage their own egos at the cost of the team. By contrast, incentives should encourage team players to help each other to optimise their collective performance. A team-oriented management style naturally also requires the management itself to set an example. Similarly, employees should treat each other with the same respect they give to external clients. This is especially true when it comes to handling conflict situations.

We have already mentioned another important cultural aspect: the need for open communication and transparent goals as well as measures and processes to realise these goals. Every employee must know the standards by which target compliance is measured internally (and which sanctions are applied for non-compliance). On every rung of the career ladder, there should be no uncertainty about the criteria for upward mobility within the company. Top management should define and formalise these criteria for the consultants. Department managers should do likewise for internal service staff.

A further important aspect of communication is that knowledge sharing must be recognised as one of the company's values. Knowledge is an asset that can advance the company as a whole. Therefore, individuals must not be allowed to hoard it for themselves in the misguided belief that "knowledge is power". Here again, this principle must be lived out from the top down. The very practice of sharing information and knowledge itself raises a consultancy's ability to innovate. Indeed, many innovations result from precisely this kind of "knowledge networking".

To solidly establish a culture of innovation, employees must have the freedom to develop new ideas beyond the scope of their concrete project work. This can, for example, take the form of PhD or MBA programs in which especially talented and successful employees are allowed to participate. At the same time, the management should encourage employees to engage in activities that serve to develop new issues and improve on existing ones. Conducting and publishing studies is a classic example. Activities of this kind must be mandatory. They should be a compulsory part of the target agreements reached between mentors and the staff they supervise. If they are, this sends a clear signal that the company is deeply committed to innovation.

Lastly, it is important for any consultancy with a global reach to live out a homogeneous corporate culture worldwide. There are several reasons why this is so. It ensures that the company shows one face to the customer. It simplifies the integration of new recruits. And it smoothes collaboration within teams of consultants, whose composition is changing all the time. The main way in which this commitment is lived out is through sharing personal knowledge and experience. This can take the form of mentorships, international exchange programs, transferring experienced staff to help start up new offices and so on. Culture cannot be decreed, it must be lived out in practice. For consultancies, this is a particularly sensitive issue as high potentials will quickly look elsewhere if they cannot identify with their current corporate culture.

The discussion so far highlights the fact that managing a consultancy cannot be compared to customary practices in the management of other industries. The most difficult task facing consultancy managers is to reconcile two apparently conflicting forces. One is the need for structures, processes, a culture and consulting services that are homogeneous throughout the world. The other is the pronounced entrepreneurial (and hence dynamic, individualistic) orientation of the company's partners and employees. Conflicting goals can certainly arise from the tension between the need for homogeneity and the commitment to entrepreneurship. Why? Because each partner – and indeed each employee – is not just part of the company as a whole, but should also be an "in-house entrepreneur". Competition within the company is a desirable condition. So each individual must be given entrepreneurial freedoms if they are to develop an entrepreneurial mindset. Only then will they maximise both personal and corporate performance.

Management's core task is, of course, to serve the interests of the entire company. It must do this by staking out the framework conditions, pursuing an appropriate staffing and recruiting policy and applying transparent controlling systems. It must also generate a culture that focuses on healthy competition, development prospects for the individual and the ability to innovate.

At the same time, the management must create and maintain structures that will enable the consultancy to grow. Structural components that facilitate growth over a long-term planning horizon must also be included. First and foremost, this means committing to highly flexible structures. Partnerships appear to be the ideal organisational form for this purpose, as they meet all the crucial requirements:

- they permit rapid growth through simple cell-division processes, even – and especially – in the context of global expansion,
- they require little organisational preparation on the mission-critical consulting side,
- they enable rapid response to new issues (e.g. by allowing teams to be reshuffled).

In addition, a partnership structure inherently creates incentives by rewarding top performance with the prospect of becoming a partner (and receiving commensurate compensation). All of which explains why strategy consultants have traditionally opted for this organisational form instead of floating their companies on the stock market.

4. Times are changing. Are consultancies fit for the future?

Partnership and growth orientation are the models that have shaped the consulting industry and facilitated its success to this day. But are they still valid as models for the future? To answer this question, we must examine three challenges that consultancies are likely to face in the near future. Firstly, clients are becoming more and more demanding as they gain experience with consultants. Secondly, competitive pressure in the consulting industry has intensified sharply. And thirdly, the battle to recruit the best people has once again broken out.

1. Let us look first at the growing demands of clients. These are rooted in the fact that many clients have already had dealings with consultancies, in some cases with a number of different companies. This puts them in a far better position to compare what each has to offer and judge the quality of their project work. Consulting experience is also being channelled into companies via another route: more and more former consultants are moving into top positions at non-consulting companies. Experience is not the only factor that is causing clients to expect more, however. Increasingly, they view consulting assignments as a normal investment. They therefore have a clear idea of the return they expect on such investments. Since fierce competition in many industries is eroding margins, clients have also become more sensitive to the price of consulting projects. As they strive for operational excellence – a focus they often "learned" from consultants in the first place – they are also committing to very strict project controlling. To put it bluntly, consultancies must adapt to new customer requirements.

2. Competition in the consulting industry has always been very intense. However, the near future should bring about a clear polarisation in the market (figure 8). Only those consultancies that position themselves clearly – as broad-liners or specialists – will thrive in the long term. Strategy consultancies that cover the entire spectrum of industries and functions can harness synergies within this portfolio. By offering their services world-wide, they are also perfectly placed to meet the needs of their global clients. The potential market for broad-liners is vast. But a full-service portfolio can only be offered worldwide by a company that is suitably dimensioned – i.e. by a company that grows. By contrast, specialists operate in niche segments to soften the force of competitive pressure. There are, however, only a limited number of niches. And growth prospects in niche markets are inevitably finite. Consultancies are unlikely to survive if they try to get the "best of both worlds". This would expose them to the need to buy in external competence for many projects. At the same time, they would find it difficult to compete with the highly specialised services offered by niche providers.

**The Strategic Decision for Management is:
Fragmentation ... or Grow**

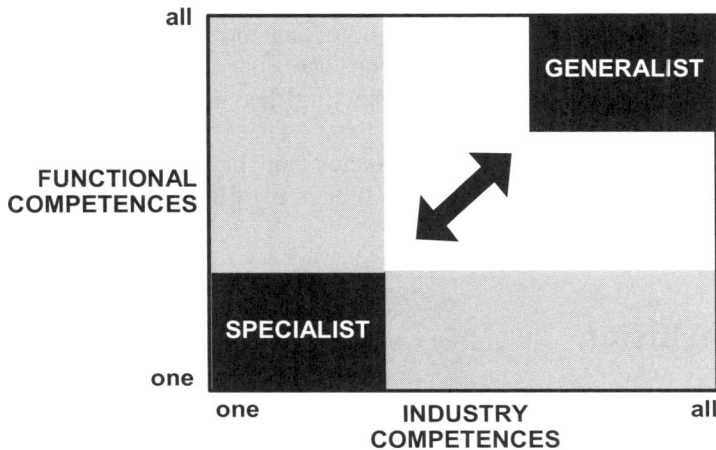

Fig. 8. Competition is going to get much fiercer – the market will split

3. For a time, the bursting of the dotcom bubble and the downbeat economy drove down the employee churn rate in the consulting market. Demand for high potentials is now rebounding, however. This is confronting consultancies with the all-too-familiar problems of the past. The number of outstanding candidates is limited. Competition from attractive multinationals, investment banks and so on is keen. Churn rates are rising once again. There is no shortage of demand for fresh ideas – and for new people to supply them. And clients now expect more for their money, as described above. Experienced consultants are therefore in great demand, on account of their social skills as much as their professional qualifications. This narrows down the group of potential candidates. Applicants are now increasingly expected to have relevant industry or consulting experience.

It appears that the management model which consultancies operate at present is certainly adequate to allow them to master the challenges ahead. Essentially, three factors substantiate this view. One is that clients are (rightly!) attaching more importance to quality than ever before. Another is that consultancies must decide clearly how they want to position themselves – and must then accept the consequences for their organisations and personnel. The third factor is that consultancies must remain an attractive employer for high potentials. All three are closely interrelated: top people, top quality and a full mastery of the relevant issues naturally go hand in hand.

It is also worth noting that the market is increasingly calling for concepts tailored precisely to specific problems, instead of standard service offerings.

Consultancies that respond to this demand can survive even in the face of growing competition. They will further establish their reputation and thus consolidate their own competitive position. This in turn will lay the basis for growth. And growth will free up cash that can be invested in new staff, new products and process innovations. This is necessary because, as market conditions continue to change, clients' sensitivity to price has the potential to erode consultancies' revenue streams. Consultancies must therefore consistently optimise their internal processes. Ultimately, clients' more exacting demands will lead to a process of natural selection amongst consulting firms. The clients will benefit by getting better value for money. Those consultancies that survive the selection process will emerge stronger and fitter. They can then look forward to sound earnings and growth prospects.

5. Conclusion

Good consultancy managers reconcile the divergent forces of internal entrepreneurship (which are both desirable and necessary) in a way that enables optimum market performance. They safeguard the reliability and neutrality of their practice. They continually invest to develop their staff and formulate fresh consulting strategies. They build up and model a culture that enables (large numbers of) new people to be integrated as an ongoing process. They give clients the guarantee that these people will consistently deliver excellent quality. While all this is happening, they themselves will still be involved in the operational business. Management will never be their sole focus. Instead, it will always be an add-on to the core activities of the consultant: acquiring and managing projects, looking after clients and solving problems.

In the light of these requirements, the partnership remains the organisational form of choice for consultancies. This form (and only this form) provides strong performance incentives, enables broad flexibility and ensures that consultancies remain independent of third-party interests.

The Third Revolution of Business Value Creation

Frank Riemensperger

1. Introduction

Today, the consulting industry is on the threshold of a dramatic market development. While the internet bubble during the late 1990s caused a short-term upheaval in the consulting industry, the challenges of today are the logical development of more long-term trends in business value creation.

As companies find themselves in a rapidly changing business environment characterised increasingly by competition on a global scale, their consulting needs are changing, too. The consulting industry is, therefore, also affected by the changing dynamics and has to adjust its business model accordingly. The following chapter will describe the profound changes that the consulting industry is facing today, highlighting the opportunities and chances that the new business environment holds and the direction in which the business model of consultancies is developing.

This chapter will first examine the development of business value creation, pointing out the different shifts in value creation over time. Today, we are facing far-reaching changes caused by the third revolution in business value creation, namely lowering the degree of vertical integration in administration processes. Secondly, the chapter will look at how the consulting market is changing as a consequence. As the client-service provider relationships change and companies increasingly expect consulting and implementation of solutions from a single source, we are witnessing the development of innovative partnerships, so-called business innovation partnerships, between companies and consultancies. Lastly, drawing from Accenture's own experience, this chapter will explain how service providers are changing to adapt to the new market dynamics.

2. The first and the second revolution of business value creation

In 1909, Ford introduced the legendary Model T. Known as the "Tin Lizzy," the commercial success of the car was not due to a product innovation; rather, the success was the result of an innovation in the business process. It was the introduction of the Fordian model of production that resulted in the first revolution of business value creation. It focused on increasing productivity through standardisation and specialised division of labour in mass production. The main idea behind standardising the production process was to minimise the overall time it took to assemble a car. The company succeeded: By 1913, Ford was able to lower the average time to assemble the chassis, suspension and engine from previously 12.5 to just 2.6 hours. This increase in productivity lowered the price of the automobiles, making them widely affordable.

While Ford focused on the optimisation of the production process, the degree of vertical integration was very high. In other words, apart from the actual assembly of the car, the company also maintained a high level of in-house production of the different parts used in the assembly. Ford aimed to keep outside contribution to the production process to a minimum: The company owned glass, steel and rubber factories which supplied the various automobile components.

Since the beginning of industrial mass production, the focus of business value creation has been on productivity. The next great shift in productivity took place in the late 1980s, when companies reduced the degree of vertical integration in production and manufacturing processes. It involved outsourcing different production steps – so-called lean production – in order to achieve cost and quality benefits. This innovation in the production process represents the second revolution of business value creation.

During the 1990s, lowering vertical integration has helped many industries to focus on expanding their product offering and – more crucially – on increasing their innovation. Outsourcing production processes to specialised suppliers has given companies the opportunity to focus more on core competencies. Product complexity is one reason for the trend towards lean production. As products become more complex, management can give less attention to the individual components, which in turn can be very complex themselves. Therefore, it no longer makes economic sense today to produce all the components in-house like Ford did. Instead, external specialists are required, who can concentrate on the production of the individual components that make up the end product. The in-depth knowledge of the specialists in turn leads to faster innovation and product development as a whole.

The automotive industry is a good example to illustrate the above-mentioned dynamics of the second revolution of business value creation. Lowering the degree of vertical integration in the manufacturing process of automobiles allowed for the high specialisation of car component suppliers. One consequence of this was that the car manufacturers could focus more on strategic issues such as brand-building, process management and administration of the supply chain, resulting in higher efficiencies.

Another consequence was the rise in quality and complexity of the automotive industry as a whole, leading to innovations such as automatic windows, airbags or ABS. Even something as simple as a car seat has undergone tremendous technological development in the last 20 years. Today, a standard car seat includes heating, electronic seat adjustments, or airbag and seatbelt detectors. A specialised seat maker can focus more readily on such innovations than the car manufacturer himself. In turn, the car manufacturer can focus more on his core business, namely on the end product and on corporate strategy.

Lowering vertical integration has led to higher quality, more product variety as well as faster innovation and product development. In many industries, lowering the degree of vertical integration has transformed the traditional value adding chain. Staying with the automotive industry as an example, it would be more appropriate to speak of a value adding "pyramid" rather than a chain, since car manufacturers concentrate on a small circle of components suppliers in order to reduce supply chain coordination. This has led to a tiered system of component suppliers, with the car manufacturers dealing mainly with the first tier suppliers that make different modules, such as dashboards or car seats. The first tier suppliers in turn deal with the second tier of subcontractors, made up of system specialists who focus on product innovation. The third and fourth tiers of suppliers produce relatively simple components or raw materials.

In Germany, the market for the car component suppliers has a volume of €57 billion. Because of the very low degree of vertical integration, the share of in-house production of car manufacturers today is on average only 25 percent. In the 1960s, this percentage was at around 70 percent. Compare this to the 9 percent share of in-house production for the Cayenne, the latest model from German carmaker Porsche. This example shows that lowering vertical integration further is reaching its limits.

For the last two to three years, companies have faced completely new challenges from changing market conditions. The current pressure to be innovative, competitive and to control costs is setting the stage for a new openness for a strategic re-positioning. This is why outsourcing operational processes as well as process re-engineering represent a high potential of business value creation for companies.

3. The third revolution of business value creation

In the light of increasing competition on a global level, companies are looking to make their internal structures more efficient and effective. The focus of value creation is shifting from manufacturing and production processes, where marginal benefits are reaching their limits, to services and administration. As in the case of the second revolution of business value creation, outsourcing administrative functions frees up capacity for companies to innovate and concentrate on their core business and on strategy.

While production costs for companies have decreased because of lowering the degree of vertical integration in production processes, administrative costs have proportionally increased as a share of overall revenue. Within the last three years, administration costs rose more significantly vis-à-vis overall revenue than production costs. Hence, it is only natural that administrative structures should become the focus of value creation.

The lowering of vertical integration in administration represents the third revolution of business value creation. Optimising the administrative processes of companies is similar to the second revolution of business value creation. Simply put, just as companies became more competitive and innovative by outsourcing production processes, the real growth potential for companies today lies in outsourcing administration processes.

While the manufacturing industry has managed to significantly lower its vertical integration, this is not yet the case in the services industry. This means that banks and insurances companies, for instance, perform most of their operations in-house – regardless of whether this is part of their core business or not. If one were to transpose this situation to the automotive industry, it would be like going back to the Fordian era, where vertical integration was high and most components were produced in-house. As this example shows, there is a tremendous potential for business value creation in the services industry.

In short: The optimisation of administrative operations is becoming increasingly important for companies, as they adjust themselves to an increasingly global business environment. There is a growing realisation that a stronger focus on the core business area is essential for companies to stay innovative and competitive. The third revolution of business value creation could therefore be an opportunity for companies that seek to create business value and to achieve a competitive edge.

4.   The potential of the outsourcing market

From a consulting point of view, the potential in the outsourcing market is tremendous. If DaimlerChrysler had been able to lower its administrative costs in 2002 by only 15 percent, the overall profit of the company would have increased by over 50 percent. This example shows that the shift of value creation to services and administration is inevitable in the coming years. According to IDC market research, the consolidated order volume in Europe for 2002 for the 20 largest transactions involving outsourcing in the area of administrative function was at €3.6 billion, of which the United Kingdom market has a share of €3.4 billion. These numbers show the potential of this market, and it is the United Kingdom that leads the way in Europe. Germany, on the other hand, has been very much lagging behind.

For German companies, this should be a signal to dramatically increase their efforts to create value. Only through innovative partnerships in the services area will companies be able to free up resources to invest in creating new jobs. Outsourcing in this respect is a chance to create jobs. Lowering the degree of vertical integration in administration of companies represents the third revolution of business value creation: Just as outsourcing production processes in the automotive industry has led to a highly specialised industry of car component supplier, there is immense potential for a new market of specialised outsourcing service providers to emerge.

The potential savings in the service and administrative functions for companies and the public sector in Germany are at around eleven percent. Only a fraction of this potentially huge outsourcing market has been opened up: Companies could save up to 11.6 cents for every euro spent – resulting in potential cost savings of up to €40 billion. This represents a largely untapped market for service providers. Currently, the share of integrated services in the consulting and technology market is at €9 billion, which means that not even a quarter of the market potential has been exhausted. The additional market potential is worth €31 billion. Again, these numbers show that the outsourcing market is a tremendous chance for consulting and technology service providers in Germany. The crucial question will be which market participant is the quickest to develop a fitting model to exploit this potential and gain the most market share.

The focus of the outsourcing market to date has been primarily on computer centres and IT services. This trend is mirrored in the distribution of the current business volume, of which IT service providers represent the largest share with 40 percent. IT implementers make up one fifth of the market volume, while IT process consultants and strategy consultants are at 10 percent and 5 percent respectively.

Given the huge potential of the business process outsourcing market, service providers will increasingly take over entire administrative processes. These operational aspects of companies, such as accounting, human resources, logistics and purchasing or IT, have one thing in common: They are vital for a company, but do not constitute the core business operations. Nevertheless, they play a major role in the cost structure – and thus the overall competitiveness – of a company.

Whereas the cost benefits achieved through lowering vertical integration in production processes are reaching their natural limits today, there is still a lot of potential business value creation in lowering the degree of vertical integration in services and administrative functions of companies. Henceforth, the market will demand more than just outsourcing of processes – the focus will increasingly be on the innovation and improvement of business processes. This is where the current consulting models are lacking, since business process competence cannot simply be acquired like car components.

The partnership between British Petroleum (BP) and Accenture is an example of successfully creating value by outsourcing entire business operations. In the face of falling oil prices and rising costs of drilling for oil in the North Sea in the late 1980s, the BP management instituted a change programme, in order to radically restructure the way the company did its business – not the core business area, but in terms of administration. In an unprecedented move at that time, the company decided in 1991 to outsource the entire finance department in partnership with Accenture.

In effect, BP proposed to pass responsibility for an entire business-critical function to its consulting firm. Until then, outsourcing had been a realm defined by such things as payroll, cafeteria support and building services; never had a corporation handed off an entire business process to a third party. A new service centre was created and over 300 BP employees transferred to Accenture. While BP retained control of financial policy, Accenture assumed responsibility for all other accounting functions, including forecasting of financial performance, joint venture accounting, preparation of management information, preparation of group and statutory accounts and the processing and payment of 15,000 invoices per month.

With a highly efficient workforce focused on services, and the leveraging of skilled professionals and advanced technology platforms such as SAP, the outsourcing arrangement led to dramatic reductions in BP's cost of accounting. In the ten years since the foundation of the service centre, BP was able to reduce its costs for the entire finance department by half. The service centre has also attracted other petroleum companies, including Talisman UK, Conoco UK and Britannia Operator.

Today, there are many other examples of companies that are successfully outsourcing entire business processes. In 2001, the Finnish mobile phone maker Nokia announced that it would outsource 300 employees of its research and development division. The employees joined TietoEnator, a leading Scandinavian technology service provider, which in turn created a new department, dedicated to overtaking most of the research and development activities on behalf of Nokia, with the aim of increasing the overall speed of product development. Another example comes from Deutsche Bank and Dresdner Bank, which announced in early 2004 that they would outsource their respective payment transactions to an external partner – Postbank. Both Deutsche Bank and Dresdner Bank expect significant savings from this outsourcing deal.

It is important to note that for companies the value created stems not merely from the outsourcing of processes; as during the second revolution of value creation, the focus is on innovation and on improving business processes as well.

5.   Consulting and implementation from a single source

As the BP example shows, companies today expect consulting and implementation from a single source. They expect pro-active project management and services, including programming and implementation, rather than mere consulting work. Instead of just a service provider, they expect a partner with shared interests.

The changes in the organisational structure of companies are mirrored by consultancies to adapt to the transforming dynamics of the business world. Consultancies are increasingly asked to take responsibility for the operation of entire business processes, leading to a new area of consulting and IT service providers.

6. Business Innovation Partnerships

We are increasingly witnessing the development of innovative partnerships between companies and consultancies. A recent Lünendonk[1] study refers to this new categorization as a "Business Innovation Partner". It involves multidisciplinary consulting and integration services, changing business processes, and partnership and shared responsibility between the company and consultancy. In the changing landscape of the consulting industry, there are only a handful of players that are capable of combining both the strategic development of new business processes and the capacity to take the responsibility and risk of running the implementation and operation. For this reason, it is likely that an oligopoly of a few, but larger, service providers will emerge in the consulting industry.

Innovation Partnerships have grown out of two management concepts: Business process outsourcing and business process re-engineering. The former emerged from the classic IT outsourcing business, namely, the outsourcing of a company's IT to a specialised external service provider. The focus of the latter is not on outsourcing but on the improvement of business processes.

The result of combining business process outsourcing with business process reengineering gives rise to innovation partnerships: The outsourced processes are restructured within the framework of a partnership between the client and the service provider, resulting in the development of competencies. Value creating processes are jointly reorganized and new innovative structures are developed. The focus is not merely on outsourcing of processes but on innovating and improving them, thereby leading to gains in efficiency and a decrease in costs.

In order to understand the concept of the Business Innovation Partner, it is useful to analyse the three components separately.

"Business": A business innovation partnership goes beyond specialisation: It covers a spectrum including strategic and IT consulting, the development of structure and processes to realise the strategy as well as the operations. Because these partnerships involve both outsourcing and re-engineering, one of the most important aspects is to ensure that the outsourced process remains in harmony with the other business areas of the company. In other words, one must understand the big picture of the entire business. This is why the innovation partner must understand all aspects of the business: strategy, structure, implementation and operations. Real value creation lies in the effective interplay of all business processes and functions of a company – hence the need for the multidisciplinary approach of a successful business innovation partner.

"Innovation": The innovation aspect of the partnership lies in re-engineering and improving business processes. This is where "thinking outside the box" becomes important in order to deal with problems in a new and innovative way to

---

[1] The new concept of a "Business Innovation Partner" was developed in a 2002 study by the Lünendonk GmbH, which regularly analyses trends in the consulting industry in Germany.

improve the way business is done. An innovation partner can bring in new ways of thinking and provide an outside perspective on how to improve established processes. In an innovation partnership, both partners benefit from a cross-fertilisation of ideas that helps to bundle the specific experience of each into co-competency.

"Partner": Trust lies at the heart of the business innovation partnership. When entire business processes are outsourced to external service providers, then companies are entrusting them with sensitive information. Investing in a business innovation partnership requires long-term commitment and trust between the partners. Successful partnerships require a sound contractual basis. In order to create co-competencies that are the necessary drivers in the improvement of business processes, both partners need to take on responsibility for the successful outcome. This implies a fair division of duties and responsibilities. Contracts should be long-term, but with enough flexibility to allow for the partnership to adjust to changing circumstances. The success of the partnership should be measured against the innovation achieved.

A business innovation partner needs to fit a certain profile in order to combine both the strategic development of new business processes and the capacity to run the implementation and operation. There are four dimensions to this profile:

- service spectrum
- operational and industry knowledge
- management quality
- global alignment

"Service spectrum": As mentioned above, companies today expect a multidisciplinary service spectrum from their innovation partners. The service spectrum includes strategic consulting for the company in the reorganisation of the business processes that are to be outsourced. During the planning stage, the allocation of organisational functions and competences between the partners is to be defined. This is where processes need to be redesigned, since most companies are still structured according to the needs of a mass market, rather than to the increasingly diversified and individualised customer needs.

Implementation is another main aspect of the service spectrum of innovation partners. This requires change management expertise from the partner to implement the reorganisation into functional operations and to make these work seamlessly with the rest of the company. Change management in itself requires a multidisciplinary approach: It involves the appropriate training of staff members concerned, the technological know-how for designing and implementing software architecture for the new business process and – most crucially – it requires the partner to guarantee the desired outcome of the redesigned business process. The operational phase following the implementation requires yet another different service spectrum. Here innovation partners need to ensure a quality service level vis-à-vis the customers, while at the same time maintaining the efficiency of the business process. This is where quality management and differentiated controlling are important.

"Operational and industry knowledge": Apart from strategic consulting and competence in implementation, innovation partners must also bring along operational and industry knowledge. Since the goal is to innovate and improve entire business processes of a company, the innovation partner must have a deep operational knowledge of the business area that it is dealing with, as well as knowledge of the industry that the company operates in.

"Management quality": The ability to manage innovation partnerships is perhaps the most crucial aspect that will determine the success or failure of a major business process reengineering. Any project as significant as innovating business processes develops a unique dynamic whose precise outcome is not always completely predictable. Building co-competencies requires a high degree of controlling and discipline from both the company and the innovation partner.

"Global alignment": For multinational companies in particular, global alignment of their innovation is a key factor for success. Global alignment means that the innovation partner is able to guarantee a constant service level regardless of location. In light of global competition, companies look for global solutions to their business challenges. Especially in outsourcing business processes, global alignment of the service partner plays a central role because it has become standard practise for companies to leverage different cost structures around the world. Highly qualified personnel in low wage countries allow companies to spread their activities globally and innovation partners need to have the global alignment to accompany this process.

7. How does the client–service provider relationship change?

In light of the changing business dynamics described above, it is clear that the traditional client-service provider relationship is changing as well. It is no longer the case that consultancies are mere service providers. The concept of business innovation partnerships shows that more is expected from them: Namely that multi-faceted consulting, implementation and operation come from a single source.

The growing number of joint subsidiaries that are created in the context of business innovation partnerships illustrates a new trend in the client-service provider relationship. One sees an increasing number of joint subsidiaries between companies and consultancies, which assume and operate outsourced business processes. These subsidiaries bundle the common interests between the partners. They integrate consulting and outsourcing capabilities across the full life cycle of business transformation.

The concept of co-competencies is another aspect of the changing client-service provider relationship. Innovation of business processes lies at the heart of business innovation partnerships that aim to optimise the degree of vertical integration of services and administrative functions – in other words, make them more efficient and effective. It is through the targeted development of co-competencies that these processes can be continually improved.

8.   How are service providers changing?

The question arises as to how the concept of the "business innovation partner" is manifested in the business strategy of the emerging group of large service providers. Analysing the structure of Accenture is an illustrative case study of how the consulting industry is changing to adjust to the market structure that it is operating in.

Accenture was formally established in 1989 as a new organisation focused on consulting and technology services related to managing large-scale systems integration and enhancing business processes. Accenture soon began offering a new breed of business integration solutions to clients – solutions that aligned organisations' technologies, processes and people with their strategies.

Accenture has a combined offering of management consulting, technology and outsourcing services. Accenture is an international company, reflected in the size of its network and in its capability to meet clients' needs on a global level. The international scope is strengthened by leveraging internet and intranet technologies, as well as global knowledge management. Continuous innovation and rapid transformation have been themes throughout Accenture's history.

The business is structured around five operating groups, which together comprise 18 industry groups serving clients in every major industry. Accenture's industry focus gives the company an understanding of industry evolution, business issues and applicable technologies, enabling it to deliver innovative solutions tailored to each client or, as appropriate, more standardised capabilities that the company offers to multiple clients.

It is worthwhile at this point to recall the aforementioned dimensions that a business innovation partner needs to have: a multidisciplinary service spectrum, operational and industry knowledge, management quality and global alignment. The full service approach requires that, in a first step, consultancies analyse the situation of the client and define the needs of the company. Forming a partnership, the partners then start the outsourcing process, implementing the changes that were identified together during the first stage, in alignment with the needs and strategy of the client. Finally, the business innovation partner also needs to manage the everyday operation of the outsourced business process.

The corporate structure of Accenture reflects its core competencies of management consulting, technology and outsourcing and closely fits the model of a business innovation partner.

In terms of consulting, Accenture addresses primarily business management and IT issues. It is during the consulting stage that individual solutions are developed in conjunction with the client. This involves identifying strategic potential and analysing how processes, for example customer relationship management or logistics, can be optimised.

The technological competence involves the development and implementation of complex technological solutions to the problems identified during the consulting stage. This is where technology-based business solutions are delivered to the clients. Accenture has specialised technology labs for the development of these solutions.

Outsourcing involves the actual operation of entire business processes, such as finance and accounting or purchasing and logistics. The crucial part is that the entire outsourcing process is undertaken together with the client – with shared risk and responsibilities. This goes back to the definition of the business innovation partnership, in which business processes are not only outsourced, but re-engineered as well, in order to improve the business process as a whole.

9.   Business model

Accenture's business model is among others marked by two main pillars: the Strategic Delivery Model and the Workforce Model. At the heart of Accenture's business is the Strategic Delivery Model (SDM). The SDM "industrialises" the delivery of technology and outsourcing solutions, thereby directly addressing the growing market brought about by the third revolution of business value creation. In particular, the SDM consists of the following elements:

- a global delivery centre network: More than 40 facilities around the globe provide a full range of technology and outsourcing services, including technology, business process outsourcing and infrastructure.
- multidisciplinary teams of professionals who possess a range of skills and experience, addressing specific client needs
- standard methodologies, tools and architectures to enhance productivity

As organisations are increasingly looking for high-quality, low cost solutions and services to boost their performances, Accenture's SDM opens up new options for organisations looking to benefit from technology and outsourcing solutions. Client projects can draw upon resources from around the globe to speed up production and lower costs. Organisations can benefit from economies of scale and distributed workloads as they outsource critical business functions. By using standard methodologies, tools, and architectures, solutions are customized and can be implemented quickly, rather than having to build new approaches from the ground up.

The SDM leverages Accenture's strengths as a global organisation, combining industry, technology and business process expertise to deliver those kinds of solutions that the changing client-service provider relationship is demanding.

10. Changing workforce model

The multifaceted approach to consulting demanded of the business innovation partners also implies that the workforce model of consultancies is changing. As the above description indicates, the cliché image of a typical consultant who develops concepts that are never implemented is undergoing change. The workforce of consultancies today must reflect the wide-ranging needs that are essential for the complex client work. It requires in-depth industry knowledge, management and skills, technological know-how and intercultural competence to address the multidisciplinary challenges of companies today. Accenture combines four distinct workforces into multidisciplinary teams:

"Consulting Workforce": Accenture's consulting workforce is involved in business consulting, process design work and the application of technologies to business. Consultants identify the needs of clients, analyse business processes that need optimisation, and design solutions that help improve clients' businesses, from strategic planning, to applying technologies to business needs and day-to-day operations.

"Solutions Workforce": Accenture Technology Solutions employees are technology specialists who build, deploy and maintain technology solutions for clients, focusing on application development, technology implementation, systems administration, and software maintenance. Solutions workforce employees mainly work on projects at client sites or delivery centres.

"Services Workforce": People working in this workforce manage and improve critical business operations for Accenture clients in areas such as IT, procurement, human resources, finance and accounting, customer contact services, insurance services and learning solutions. The majority of the people who work in the outsourcing business are involved in client operations. They are responsible for providing long-term outsourcing services to one or multiple clients. They implement, manage, and ultimately transform the day-to-day activities associated with the above mentioned business functions.

"Enterprise Workforce": These people manage and operate Accenture's own business functions, and support client teams while working in areas such as Finance, Human Resources, Information Technology, Legal, and Marketing. They perform a variety of jobs, which are mainly situated in locations where they are most relevant to the work being performed. These locations are in any of the 48 countries in which Accenture operates, and may be at a client site, in a shared services centre (e.g. a call centre or a billing centre), or in an Accenture office.

Our business is a people business. The knowledge we create, the skills and the experience of our people contribute most to the success of our clients. Our most important challenge is, therefore, how to combine the strengths of our three client facing workforces with their different career paths and skills. In this context, two aspects have to be considered: Our way to "balance" our workforces and our company culture in combination with the leadership of our executives.

The different career models of the workforces are tailored to the relevant skill tracks. Each workforce therefore requires a clear value proposition associated with working for Accenture. Depending on the client engagement, the different workforces combine as a team to cooperate on various projects. The advantage of the team approach is that a strong exchange of experience takes place between the workforces, thereby adding value to both Accenture and its clients.

Achieving a balance between the workforces is an important aspect of the management of this model. This is among the reasons why Accenture's top management in the geography ASG (Austria, Switzerland, Germany) – the so-called "Geographic Council" – mirrors the workforces. Furthermore, all the workforces are managed by the same HR organisation within the Enterprise Workforce. Accenture emphasizes the relevance of internal communications for all of the workforces; or in the case that the communication is only of interest to one particular workforce, it is provided in such a way, that the relevant points of interest for other workforces are accessible to them, too.

One of the key points is, however, that the workforce model can only be effective if the same core values and company culture are shared across the workforces and if there is a corresponding leadership development.

11. Accenture's company culture

Accenture builds on a set of core values that we have long embraced and consistently strived to implement in our daily work:

- Client Value Creation
- One Global Network
- Integrity
- Stewardship
- Best People
- Respect for the Individual

These core values have served as a compass to guide the company's decision-making at a company and at an individual level. The ongoing commitment to these values is necessary to ensure that we will operate with the highest ethical standards and achieve our vision to become one of the world's leading companies, bringing innovations to improve the way the world works and lives. Accenture also strives to create value for its clients. In so doing, it is essential that we conduct our business activities in a manner that is lawful and fair, with the highest level of integrity, to our people, our clients, other stakeholders and our communities.

To sum up: Accenture structures its workforce model according to the complex needs that are required by the changing client-service provider relationship. While each of the workforces exhibits the in-depth, specialised knowledge that clients expect from a business innovation partner, the workforces share a common company culture and core values.

12. Leadership within Accenture

Given it's workforce model, Accenture is committed to developing strong leaders at all levels of the company. The company has therefore put in place a Leadership Development Programme. The objective of this programme is continuous investment in the improvement of leadership capabilities to support strategic business objectives. The Accenture Leadership Development Programme has been designed by global and local human resources experts in cooperation with a Partner Steering Committee. The Leadership Development Programme was established in the ASG region in September 2002.

The programme is driven by the Accenture Leadership Statement, which defines the imperatives for a successful leader and leadership roles relevant to Accenture. This Leadership Statement has been translated into a leadership competence matrix defining relevant behaviours and skills per level and leadership role. The development vehicles have been consequently designed on the basis of the defined competences, and integrated into the existing and new HR processes.

The Leadership Statement represents a formal definition of leadership and the corresponding behaviours Accenture aspires to achieve as an organisation. It describes the three leadership contributions that have been defined for Accenture - Value Creator, People Developer and Business Operator (which relate directly to the company's strategic imperatives). The statement is used as a basis for evaluating performance, and serves as a common framework for career management decisions. The Leadership Statement also includes definitions of Accenture's six core values.

Business results are essential but not sufficient to be a successful Accenture leader. There needs to be a balance across the three areas of leadership (Value Creator, People Developer, Business Operator). The definition of leadership is intended to encourage leaders to develop their own authentic leadership style. They are expected to develop their own leadership beliefs into their own 'teachable point of view', which they articulate for their teams. By having this programme in place, we are able to develop the leaders we need in order to balance our workforces.

13. Conclusion

The third revolution of business value creation has far-reaching consequences for the consulting industry. With the focus of value creation shifting to administration processes, the focus of consulting companies must adjust itself as well. With consultancies being increasingly asked to take responsibility for designing and operating entire business processes, we are witnessing the development of business innovation partnerships between companies and consultancies.

Given these trends, it is likely that a few, large service providers will emerge that can offer multifaceted consulting, implementation and operations services from a single source. Accenture, with its workforce and service delivery model, is among those few players that are in a strong position to benefit from the changing dynamics of the consulting market, brought about by the third revolution of business value creation. Delivering a wide range of services from a single source requires special efforts with regard to the human resources functions and the leadership skills in such companies.

References

Fink, Dietmar/Köhler, Thomas/Scholtissek, Stephan (2004): Die dritte Revolution der Wertschöpfung: Mit Co-Kompetenzen zum Unternehmenserfolg, Econ Verlag, Munich.

Consulting Management in a Multi-Disciplinary Advisory Firm

Wolfgang Zillessen

1. Introduction

In today's demanding and often volatile business environment top managers are confronted with increasingly complex business issues. The definition of global operating models for defined business segments, the evaluation and execution of major company transactions, or the design and implementation of cross-border business restructuring require the knowledge, experience, and collaboration of specialists from many different disciplines.

Companies looking for outside advice on any such transaction either source and integrate best-in-class specialist know-how from dedicated strategy boutiques, operations improvement consultancies, tax advisors and corporate finance experts, or they rely upon a multi-disciplinary firm assuming that it will integrate the different skills for a given business problem.

As the world has become more global, complex and fast changing, one would assume that there is plenty of ground for multi-disciplinary firms to exist. The reality instead is very different. The number of firms able to offer and integrate different disciplines such as management consultancy, tax advisory, corporate finance, and assurance is rather small. Few of the existing firms are large and global in presence, although several other advisory firms have made commitments to their clients recently to provide a wider scope of services in the future.

There are several reasons why the number of global multi-disciplinary services firms is relatively small:

- **The quality challenge**: Each discipline assurance, tax, corporate finance, and consulting needs to strive for the highest degree of quality and integrity. Sustaining superior performance in any discipline is the prerequisite for an integrated multi-disciplinary firm to achieve a competitive edge over focused single-discipline advisory firms.
- **The culture challenge**: There is no dispute that the cultures required to lead and develop auditors, tax advisors, management consultants and corporate finance professionals are quite diverse. Only partnerships with the highest ethical standards and sound professional skills are able to create a culture of mutual respect and support.
- **The value creation challenge**: With the boom in technology services since 1995 the focus of many consulting practices has shifted from primarily advisory services to IT and implementation services. Several multi-disciplinary

firms carved out and sold these IT oriented advisory services in order to create value for their partners and to reduce their equity risk resulting from big and risky IT projects in a fast-changing business environment. During and shortly after the eBusiness bubble, a number of firms sold their consulting businesses to stock-listed IT services companies. Several former multi-disciplinary firms are apparently planning to return to a "full-service" model once they are free from separation-related non-compete agreements.

- **The independence challenge**: When advisory firms offer a broad range of services, they must adhere to strict policies and processes of risk and independence management at national and global level. Selecting clients, determining the services they offer, defining the engagement terms for the specified services, and addressing engagement risks early are fundamental considerations for ensuring independence towards their clients and avoiding conflict of services.

- **The regulatory challenge**: One of the key tasks for stock market listed companies as well as for their advisors is to rebuild the confidence of the public in the capital market system, in financial reporting, and in corporate governance. Multi-disciplinary advisory firms play a key role in both the development of regulatory codes and national legislations, and in effective implementation. The Sarbanes-Oxley Act in the United States and the proposed 8th Company Law Directive in the European Union clarify the limitations on the provision of non-audit services to audit clients. There is the clear expectation that individual national regulations will become more coherent in the interest of investors in global companies.

This chapter describes objectives and performance of multi-disciplinary advisory firms and how they operate in order to meet the challenges that are clearly set for their existence.

2. Defining the multi-disciplinary advisory firm

Multi-disciplinary firms are typically built around a number of functions, which are principally in the areas of

- Assurance services
- Enterprise risk management services
- Tax compliance and advisory services
- Financial advisory services
- Management advisory services / consulting

Each of these functions requires a distinct identity in order to attract and develop talent and professional capabilities, and to serve clients. Figure 1 shows a typical set up of functions and services for a multi-disciplinary firm.

Sample MDF Service Portfolio

Strategy & Organisation	Human Capital	Corporate Finance	Taxation
• Corporate Strategy • Organizational Change and Transformation • Customer/Market Strategies • IT Strategy • Operational Excellence • Program Leadership • Finance Transformation	• Actuarial and Insurance Consulting • Employee Benefits • Human Resource Strategies • Interim Management, Search and Selection • Risk Management • Health Plan Consulting	• M&A / Due Diligence • Transaction Services • Restructuring Services • Valuation Services • Business Modelling • Dispute Consulting and Forensic	• Tax Planning • Corporate Transactions • Transfer Pricing • Cross-Border Structuring • Capital Markets • Indirect Taxes

Operations Management	Enterprise Applications	Assurance	Enterprise Risk Services
• CRM Strategy • Customer Analytics • Product Innovation • Sales Force Effectiveness • Customer Service • Collaborative Commerce • Sourcing and Procurement • Supply Chain Strategy and Operations	• Process reengineering, design and benchmarking • Feasibility and business cases • Application design and implementation • Application program management	• Attest services • Company valuation • GAAP and IAS Conversion • Corporate Governance Services	• Capital Markets • Internal Audit and Control Assurance • Regulatory Consulting • Securitization Consulting

Fig. 1. Sample of MDF service portfolio

Typically, many client relationships in a multi-disciplinary services firm are single-function focussed at the beginning. Over time clients may recognize the value and potential of a broader service offering and receive services from several functions. While these services may not be strongly interdependent in the first place, a key objective for multi-disciplinary firms is to provide integrated solution offerings to their clients and support them in major company transactions and transformation projects.

Figure 2 explains the principle concept of a multi-disciplinary services model. While capabilities continue to come from different functions, they are combined to solve complex business problems. Moving up the pyramid clearly mandates additional emphasis at each of these levels with the local and regional regulatory and corporate governance environment. To avoid potential conflicts of interest and compliance issues, it is imperative for multi-disciplinary firms to operate strict procedures with engagement management responsibilities for clients.

While strong independence of audit services is vital to its existence, the knowledge and experience of specialists in areas such as information technology, security, internal controls, capital markets, taxation and actuarial services can be a prerequisite for high-quality audits in today's environment of increasingly complex technology, transactions, and business structures.

Objective thinking is, however, characteristic of all functions. Just as important as independence is vital to high-quality audit services, objectivity is a precursor to delivering all types of advisory services. Conflicts can arise from combinations of services such as strategy consulting, corporate finance, employee benefits programmes, or internal control reviews, if these are not carefully mastered.

In addition to objectivity and cross-functional quality measures, function-specific quality assurance must be designed to address the unique considerations and characteristics associated with delivering different types of advisory services.

Multi-Disciplinary Services Model

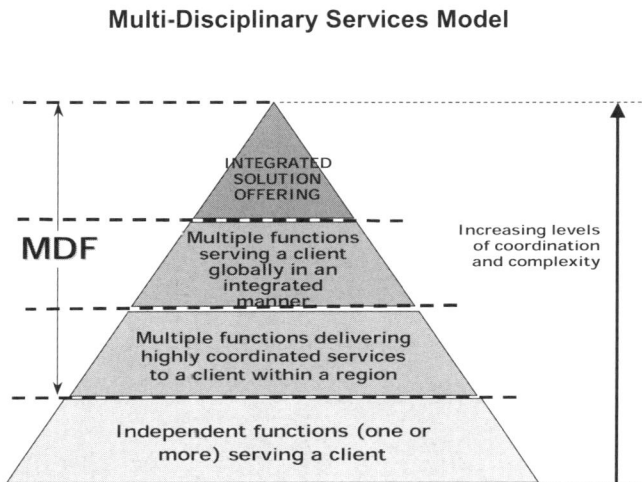

Fig. 2. Multi-disciplinary services model

As we see at the top of the pyramid in figure 2, multi-disciplinary firms are targeting to serve clients in complex business transactions when clients do not just require a combination of different functional services, but when integrated solutions with sound methodologies provide benefits in terms of speed and value for money to their clients. There are some typical business situations when multi-functional services are sought by clients:

- **Corporate Restructuring Programmes**: When major restructuring and cost reduction programs are launched, a combination of sound process and industry knowledge, a solid understanding of its business portfolio and possible divestures and carve-outs may be as important as to understand how these programmes will be reflected on a company's balance sheet and how they can be communicated to capital markets. In addition, information technology can be a driver or a roadblock in achieving a significant improvement in business performance, which makes IT expertise a prerequisite for the design and implementation of restructuring initiatives.
- **Supply Chain Network Optimisation**: Globalisation of businesses, mass customisation of products and the opening of new markets in Asia and other world regions requires companies to continuously monitor and review their supply chain networks, and to make deliberate decisions about the selection, (re)location and consolidation of production and assembly sites.

The optimisation of production networks, product flows, and distribution and transportation structures certainly requires a sound analysis of material, value, and information flows. Valuations for alternative site locations must be conducted and local employment laws are to be taken into account in order to implement any site relocation or consolidation programme. In addition, the restructuring of supply chain networks allows companies to review their global tax structure. Different instruments are available to optimise and shift the ownership of assets, risks, and business functions along the value chain to incur profits at tax efficient locations. Only integrated supply chain network and tax planning can lead to reduced supply chain costs and improved profit margins at corporate level.

- **End-to-End Acquisition and Merger Integration**: When companies decide to realign their business portfolio and divest existing businesses or make acquisitions that fit their strategic core, significant business transactions are usually at stake. Carve-outs might lead to management buy-outs, share splits or competitive sales auctions requiring advisory support for vendor due diligence reports, management equity plans and company valuations.

The acquisition and integration of target companies require corporate finance, business consulting and tax services including finance and business due diligence, tax structuring, purchase price accounting, transaction closing, day-one merger integration planning and support.

Figure 3 describes "end-to-end acquisition and merger integration" as an example of scope and subject expertise required to manage complex business transactions.

End-To-End Acquisition and Merger Integration

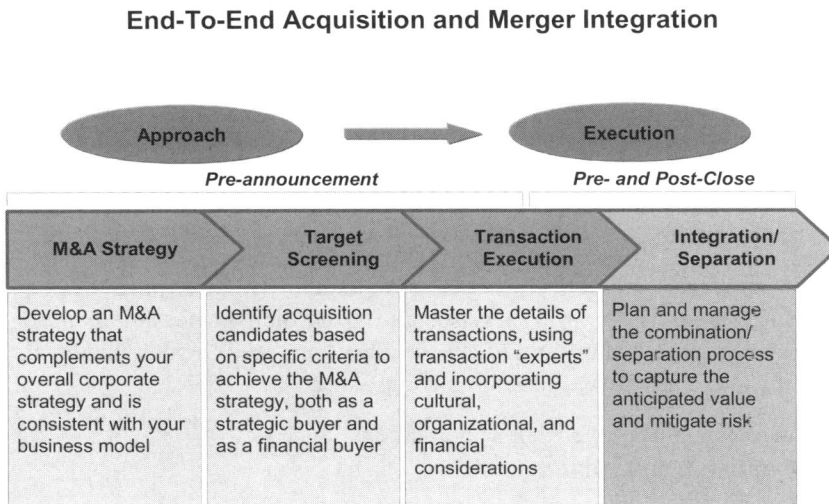

Fig. 3. End-to-end acquisition and merger integration

While complex business transactions sound like an ideal case for multi-disciplinary services firms, they are certainly competing for such engagements against a combination of single-discipline companies when clients undertake the integration effort themselves or when the combination of single-discipline offerings would provide better quality of services compared to an integrated multi-disciplinary service offering.

Given the size and complexity of a multi-disciplinary business, these firms need to master two key challenges in order to be successful in the market and out-compete single-disciplinary firms in complex business transactions:

- **Go-to-Market approach**: How to ensure that global clients are served with a consistent set of high-quality, often distinct services around the globe?
- **Operating Model**: How to ensure that individual functions can provide their services independent of any other functions and without creating potential conflicts?

3.   Go-to-market approach

The broad set of service offerings from multi-disciplinary services firms is as much an opportunity as it is a challenge, and it could easily turn into a threat if not managed properly. The challenge lies in the wide scope of services and distinct skills and independence issues for individual functions, which themselves are already pretty large and broad. At the same time, many advisory assignments cover a wide range of geographies and require rigid coordination across regions and countries in order to cope with the specific business, legal and regulatory requirements across the globe.

There are basically three dimensions to each services organisation that must play together in order to serve clients appropriately:

- **Competencies**: Strong functional capabilities such as logistics management and warehousing, research and development, financial accounting, and customer management

- **Functional services**: Originally a set of competencies that require a specific education such as an MBA or tax advisor and grow their professionals along a dedicated career path. Many multi-disciplinary services firms cluster their competencies into a set of five functions comprising

  - Assurance and Enterprise Risk Management,
  - Tax Compliance and Advisory,
  - Corporate Finance,
  - Management Consulting, and
  - Human Capital Management.

While all professionals must decide and follow the specific training and career path for one dedicated function, more senior people starting at project leader level and cutting across much of the partner group need to acquire some overlapping basic knowledge from different functions in order to be able to involve and coordinate with their colleagues from other functional services on multi-disciplinary business issues.

- **Industry practices**: These practices develop focussed knowledge about the dynamics of a specific industry or industry segment. They shape service offerings from any given function to the specific challenges of industry segments. They develop specific industry programmes based upon industry thought leadership, and they structure and assemble multi-disciplinary offerings for the advisory market. The collaboration between industries and functions also creates a specific challenge for multi-disciplinary firms. While industries have a key impact on management consulting and corporate finance in order to serve clients at all, they have a lesser, but not negligible impact on assurance and tax advisory.

The diagram in figure 4 explains how the different dimensions of a services organisation play together in serving the market. While competencies, functions, and industries coordinate internally through a matrix organisation, they must operate towards the market through a clearly defined channel approach.

"Go-To-Market" Approach in Multi-Disciplinary Firms

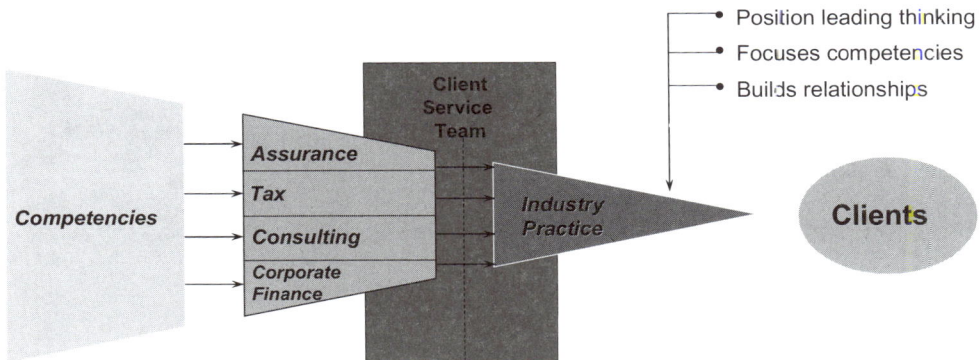

Fig. 4. "Go-to-market" approach in multi-disciplinary firms

While traditional single-disciplinary services firms may allow themselves to serve the market through competencies and industries, the broad service offerings from multi-disciplinary firms definitely create more complexity and require a clear "go-to-market" approach through industries.

Industries in this case are not only responsible for shaping service offerings to the specific needs of industry segments and for serving clients through industry thought leadership. They take decisions on industry and client programmes and on the scope of services to be offered to individual clients in the light of regulatory requirements and in avoidance of possible conflicts of interest. In addition, they identify lead client service partners from the different functions able to best serve the client with the specific set of services.

Such mechanisms must be put in place both at country as well at global level. They proactively manage a firm's client portfolio and develop decisions and distinctions between serving of audit and non-audit clients (see figure 5).

Clients & Markets

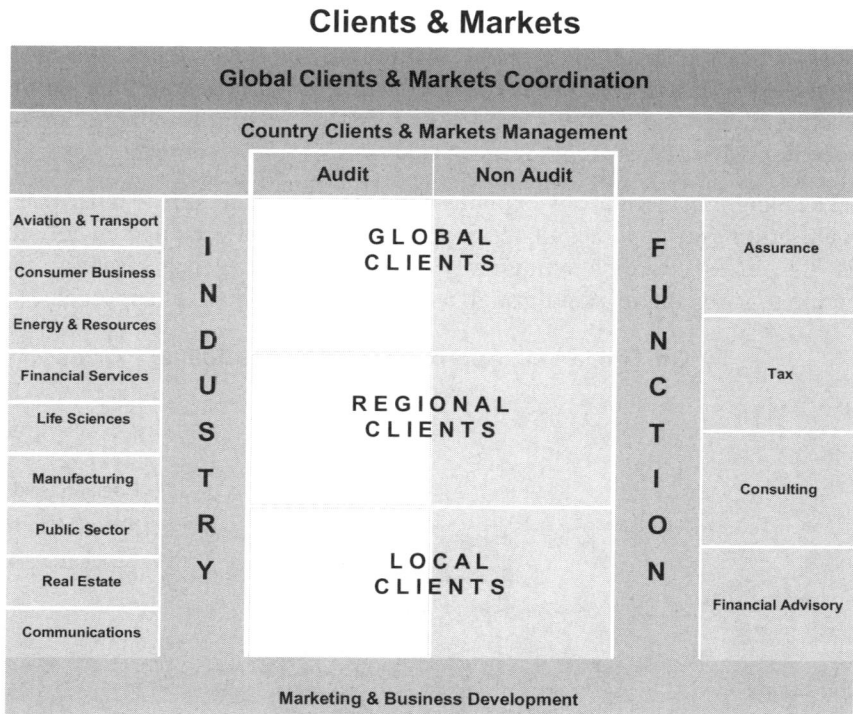

Fig. 5. Clients & markets

4. Operating model

When comparing the operating models of single-discipline and multi-disciplinary services firms, the key difference lies in the implementation of processes,

- to assure the client and the public that neither the firm nor its professionals have any financial, business or other relationships with audit and corporate finance clients

- to comply with limitations on the provision of some non-audit services to audit clients and to avoid any conflict of interest between management consulting, corporate finance, and tax services.

Maintaining independence from audit clients and avoiding conflicts of interest across the different competencies and functions entails more than compliance with rules and regulations. As recent corporate scandals have demonstrated, perception can become reality in today's environment. Multi-disciplinary services firms must consider how their independence is perceived.

Legislation, regulations, and professional guidance can in fact mandate independence, but the appearance of independence cannot always be dictated by rules. It is dependent on professionals who act with sound judgement, objectivity, healthy scepticism, and integrity. Beyond complying with applicable rules and regulations, professionals must be perceived as being independent by clients and the investing public.

In order to cope with these requirements, a multifaceted approach of independence safeguards is required including an expansive consultation network, policies, financial interest tracking systems, and appropriate monitoring mechanisms:

- **Global Consultation Network**: Multi-disciplinary firms provide a global consultation network that covers all country firms and all services. A network of a global lead partner for independence, supported by a staff of independence specialists and a network of country partners responsible for independence measures, monitors compliance with independence policies and regulations. In addition, this global independence network is a consultation resource for all professionals when independence issues arise.

- **Independence Policies, Procedures, and Training**: A multi-disciplinary firm maintains a comprehensive set of written independence policies for all professionals independent of their specific functional dedication. These materials are compliant with all applicable rules and regulations and provide documentation for use in training of partners and staff.

- **Tracking of Financial Investments**: To help ensure the independence of staff and partners, multi-disciplinary firms use proprietary information systems to track the financial interests of its professionals. Each partner and other senior staff members must enter all their financial investments into an electronic tracking system. Each person's portfolio can then be checked against a list of clients that require independence to facilitate timely identification and resolution of conflicts.

- **Scope of Service**: Multi-disciplinary firms run strict global client and engagement acceptance policies and processes to ensure independence and to identify conflict of interest issues early on. An individual client service partner must verify that the services he will provide are permissible under applicable independence policies. In addition, each individual partner is required to confirm compliance with independence policies each year, and many firms, by way of their own policies, can exercise disciplinary action ranging from reprimand to termination of contracts with professionals who do not comply with independence policies.

- **Partner Compensation**: To further ensure that audit partners focus on their primary responsibility to provide high-quality audit services, many multi-disciplinary firms have policies that forbid audit partners from receiving direct financial incentives to sell products and services to their audit clients, other than those related to audit, review, and attestation. While this limits cross-selling across different competencies for obvious reasons, there are generally no issues associated with providing partners with incentives to sell services to clients when they do not participate in the audit of these clients.

5. How to grow a successful consulting business in an MDF environment

In general, the critical success factors for developing and growing a successful consulting business in a multi-disciplinary practice are not materially different from single-discipline consulting firms. Additionally, the broader set of services enables a consulting business to cope with more complex business issues and allows such firms to benefit from cross-selling through a wider network of client relationships albeit limited by independence rules and policies as mentioned above.

On the other hand, if not managed properly, a multi-disciplinary environment can present a set of additional challenges to a consulting business. Some key issues to deal with include:

- **Branding & Marketing**: While an assurance and a tax advisory business is traditionally less aggressive and less visible in marketing and brand development, management consulting businesses require a much more proactive approach and must drive new themes into the marketplace on a regular basis. In addition, there are significant legal limitations for auditors and tax advisors in many jurisdictions.

- **Partner Role**: Assurance partners carry a significant personal responsibility in their attest work and cannot be compromised by organisational hierarchies or any governing body within a multi-disciplinary firm. On the contrary, partners in management consulting rely with their judgement much more on practice structures and do not necessarily bear similar personal liabilities in their professional work. These differences often create a challenging balancing act between a more direct and proactive leadership style that suits a management consulting business in contrast to an assurance business where the personal responsibility of an individual partner cannot be compromised.

- **Business Volatility**: Due to its nature, assurance and tax advisory businesses are significantly more stable than management consulting. Once a team has been assembled for an audit client, there is a joint interest to have the team learn and focus on one client for a number of years. Even though several firms have put rotation policies in place, lead partners and teams stay with the same client over a number of years. Similar characteristics apply to the tax advisory business, while management consulting and corporate finance businesses are significantly more volatile and require more sophisticated operational processes in areas such as staff scheduling, assignment management, and operational controlling.

- **Career Development**: A multi-disciplinary firm offers a broad set of individual career opportunities and develops professionals with very different functional expertise. While some commonality exists in personnel administration and related processes, it is important for such firms to develop professionals along distinct career expectations in each function of their business and to cope, for example, with different career stage models and compensation structures.

Multi-disciplinary firms are certainly a different animal than pure-play management consulting firms. While they offer by the nature of their business a significantly wider range of services, their success depends on meeting the quality standards of single-discipline firms and finding the balance both in operations and management philosophy to support highly regulated businesses as well as more volatile financial and management advisory services.

The Changing Balance of Power in the Consulting Market and Its Effects on Consulting Firms

Ansgar Richter[1]

1. Introduction

In a recent interview, a partner in one of the major consulting firms told me: "I joined this firm only eight years ago, but I have the feeling that this is not any longer the firm I entered". When asked what had changed, he said: "Through the downturn of the last few years, our company has become so much more business-like. I never thought about my firm as a business. For me, it had always been an institution which had to be nurtured and upheld for its own sake. We did not even have anything like a strategy, and nobody thought we needed one. Now, everybody is talking about revenue streams, cost controls and utilisation ratios. To be sure, there are many good aspects to that. I believe that the firm is now on a much sounder footing than it used to be, and as the market is picking up again, we can reap the fruits of many of the measures we have taken. But I do not think this firm will ever return to the old regime, and somehow, that is sad". Similar sentiments can be heard frequently when talking to senior consultants from a cross-section of firms.

From their work in the industries of their clients, consultants understand that the shape of firms reflects the realities of their industries, and of the economy at large. They know that in times of economic crisis and adverse industry conditions, companies in many industries tend to reduce the size of their head offices, cut perks, and eliminate staff positions that add little value. Yet for consultants, it may be difficult to see how the conditions in their own sector affect the structure of their own organisations. In this chapter, I look into these transmission mechanisms.

My overall argument is that the organisational changes that we see among consulting firms reflect a fundamental shift in the relative abilities of consultants and clients to appropriate the rents generated from consulting services. As the balance of power shifts away from consultants in favour of clients, lower rents are left for the internal stakeholders of consulting firms (employed professionals, partners, support staff). In a tighter market environment, consultants adopt new strategies – they seek to occupy new market niches, which had hitherto appeared unattractive – and develop organisational forms that match these new strategic

---

[1] In preparing this chapter, I have benefited greatly from discussions with and comments by Michael Graubner, Katrin Lingelbach, and above all, Jonathan Day.

requirements. As a result, we see the landscape of consulting organisations changing. During the boom period of the 1950s to the early 1970s, the so-called professional partnership model had become the dominant organisational form for consulting firms. In the 1980s and 1990s, the professional partnership model was complemented by managed professional businesses. Under the current pressures in the consulting market, the bifurcation between these two types of firms is increasing. Weaker players are increasingly excluded from entering the circle of professional partnership firms; they will seek to establish business models of a more operational type, diversify away from consulting, or leave the market altogether. Overall, the shift away from the consultants to clients in terms of their relative ability to appropriate value will lead to fundamental changes in the shape of consulting firms. The old order in the consulting market will never be established again.

2. The changing balance of power in the consulting market

Standard economics tells us that the purpose of the transformation of input factors into outputs is to generate added value. Customers buy goods or services because their value exceeds the price they need to pay for them. That price, in turn, has to exceed the total costs of the input factors (supplies, financial capital, labour) plus any additional costs such as taxes required to generate the outputs concerned in the first place, at least if the producer is to work profitably. As a result, under normal circumstances both buyers and suppliers of goods and services reap rents, in the form of a share of the total value added by the generation and consumption of goods and services. Shifts in the distribution of value between suppliers and buyers, however, are indicative of the relative ability of these various parties to appropriate value. Market conditions are among the main drivers of such shifts.

With respect to the consulting market, the balance of power between consultants as the providers of consulting services and clients as buyers has shifted significantly over the past few years, and indications are that this process is likely to continue. Overall, the shift has benefited clients, and reduced the relative ability of consultants to appropriate a share of the value generated by the rendering of their services. In this context, it is worth considering both the demand and the supply side factors that have contributed to this development.

2.1   General economic conditions and the demand for consulting services

As the market for consulting services matures, it becomes apparent that demand in the sector is ultimately driven by general economic conditions. During the boom years of the 1950s to the early 1970s, the provision of consulting services to the management of large industrial companies and commercial organisations was essentially a new type of service. Although consulting has its historical roots in the late 19th century, it was during the second half of the 20th century that consulting firms of a hitherto unknown scale emerged, which were able to capture the gains from experience and scale, and provide advice to the leading companies of their time. To use the life cycle concept, the market for consulting services was in a stage of takeoff and growth. Clients were still toying around with whether to use the help of consultants or not. The first Harvard Business Review article – usually a good indicator of what is going on in the minds of executives – on how to engage professional service providers, and one that is still worth reading, was written by Warren J. Wittreich in 1966.

In the wake of the oil shocks of 1973/74 and 1978/79 and faltering economic conditions, the consulting industry showed the first signs of weakness. Many industrial clients already had some experience in using the help of consultants and were reluctant to spend further money on a service whose long-term economic impact was still unproven. Alternative sources of demand (and growth) were not in sight as yet.

During the 1980s and part of the 1990s, however, heavy restructuring in the wake of the economic recessions fuelled the demand for consulting services. This observation seems to contradict the above argument that growth in the economy at large should ultimately drive demand for consulting services. However, even during the 1980s, consulting had not fully penetrated the corporate economy. The 1980s mark a generational change in the corporate economy of the Western world. Fundamental developments such as privatisation and liberalisation, the growing competition from the East Asian economies, and the increased importance of environmental sustainability, are just some of the changes that characterise this decade. In this period of increased uncertainty and change, managers were looking for the help of advisors who gave them guidance on how to master the challenges of the day. During the 1990s, general economic growth fuelled the demand for consulting services. With the benefit of hindsight, we recognise that during this period extraordinary factors, such as the restructuring of the German economy following unification, the opening of the East European markets, and the e-business boom, helped to lift the demand for consulting services beyond what it would otherwise have been.

Overall, the past fifty to sixty years have been a success story for the consulting industry. Despite a concomitant increase in supply, strong growth in the demand for consulting services has kept profit margins in the consulting industry way above the average of other industries. While many industry observers lament about the worsening economic conditions for consulting firms, it should not be forgotten that consulting firms have enjoyed an unusually long period of economic prosperity which few other sectors can claim.

Over the past five to ten years, however, the consulting industry has begun to enter a phase of maturity. In this situation, the demand for consulting services is likely to follow the general state of the economy more closely than used to be the case when the industry was in its infancy. At least in the Western societies, the consulting market may amplify general economic conditions, but the one will not be dissociated from the other. Growth rates in the economy at large, however, are likely to remain at the level of lower single digit figures. In this situation, it is hard to see how average growth rates in the demand for consulting services could possibly reach the double-digit figures which they reached during the 1990s.

There are several reasons for the slower growth in the demand for consulting services in the Western world, two of which – the slower growth of the economy as a whole and the maturity of consulting services as a service concept – have been discussed already. A third and important reason is that substitutes for consulting services at competitive prices have emerged. As an example, with greater availability of information through the development of the internet and other technologies, the role of consultants as generators of primary data has clearly diminished. Similarly, the availability of standard methods such as econometric tools and other analytical techniques means that the need for consultants to engage in the analysis part of many consulting projects has dropped; in some cases this can even be outsourced to third-party providers. The point here is not that these new resources – data, tools, techniques, etc. – render consultants entirely unnecessary; in many cases, we see consultants use these tools more proficiently than clients. However, consulting can be understood as a series of steps in a value chain which starts with project set-up and scoping, data gathering and analysis, followed by the development of new concepts, their communication to the client, and implementation. The relative importance of consultants in *some* of the steps of the value chain is decreasing, thus reducing the overall demand for the activities provided by consultants. At least in strategy consulting, the value chain is in a process of disintegration (Schmidt and Vogt, 2004).

In addition to the limits in the *quantity* of the demand for consulting services, the *type* of services that clients demand is in a process of change. Today, clients have the power to push through very specific expectations with respect to aspects such as the composition of individual teams, project start dates, and so on. They tend to expect more experienced and slightly older consultants, and are less prepared to pay the kinds of fees they used to for younger graduates who have yet to learn their trade. They also look for consulting services of a more innovative type which embodies cutting-edge thinking, advanced analytical capabilities, and an in-depth understanding of industry dynamics. They concentrate their demand on those providers who can deliver these types of services, implying that others will come away empty-handed.

Overall, there are no reasons to expect the need for consulting services will vanish entirely. Consulting has established itself as an important sector of the economy; it will stay that way. However, the average growth rate of that sector is likely to be more moderate – closer to that of other mature industries – than used to be the case for much of the post-war history.

2.2   Supply of consulting services

The development of the demand for consulting services described above is closely mirrored by the changes on the supply side. As demand increased after

World War II, and clients began to take an interest in a new type of service beyond the traditional offerings directed towards enhancing operational efficiency, consulting firms of a new type including Arthur D. Little, A.T. Kearney, Booz Allen Hamilton, and McKinsey & Company began to prosper (Kipping, 2002). Within a mere 15 years, these firms, which had by no means always been successful (see for the example Kahn's (1986) book on Arthur D. Little) were able to replace the consulting firms that had dominated the market during the 'first wave' of the industry's development, such as the 'big four' firms in Britain (AIC, Production Engineering, PA Consulting, and Urwick, Orr & Partners).

Three Waves of Consulting

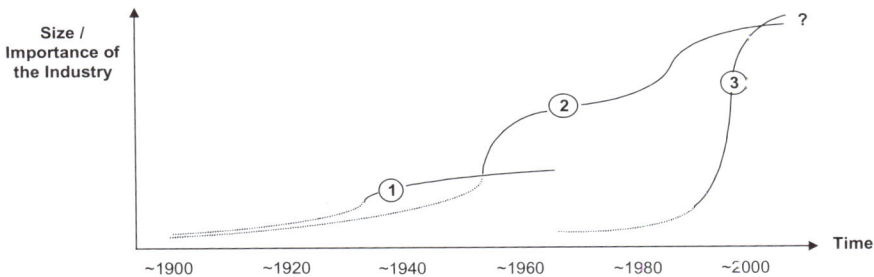

Fig. 1. Three waves of the development of the consulting industry

The firms of the 'second wave' thrived on two interrelated successes. First, they shifted the focus of their services away from areas that could legitimately be regarded as the remit of functional specialists, such as engineers or accountants. They were able to develop meaningful concepts and approaches in the area of general management, including strategy and organisation. Through this change, they were also able to shift their focus towards top managers as their primary target clients, rather than functional specialists who would only control a portion of the overall revenues and costs of their organisations. Second, these firms developed organisational processes and structures now known as the professional partnership model (see below) which proved not only stable and expendable, but optimally geared towards supporting the type of service these firms were offering.

Attracted by the success of these firms, many other firms began to enter the industry and offer their services to clients. In 1963, Bruce Henderson, formerly with Arthur D. Little, founded the Boston Consulting Group (BCG). He was also involved in other ventures, such as the joint venture with the Italian entrepreneur Gennaro, the company at which Roland Berger received his first training until he set up his own firm in Munich in 1967. Many consultancies were established by former employees of already existing consulting firms. Bain & Company was founded by William Bain, a former BCG consultant, in 1973. The L.E.K. partnership was founded in 1983 as a spin-off from Bain; Braxton Associates emerged in 1976 as a spin-off from BCG but was later acquired by Deloitte Touche. Other firms resulted from the bundling of existing capabilities, such as Groupe Bossard in France, created in 1962 through the merger of Organisation Pierre Michel (created in 1946) and Organisation Yves Bossard, set up in 1956 (Hendersen and Boscheck, 1991). Not all of the firms founded during the 1950s and 1960s survived. Overall, however, the margins that could be gained in the consulting industry attracted a growing number of entrants aiming to take a share of the market.

By the early 1980s, the growth of the consulting industry had become sufficiently noticeable to attract firms from adjacent industries to push into the consulting market. With low barriers to entry in consulting, virtually all major accounting firms, plus a number of firms from the IT and other industries, began to add consulting to their service offerings. On the basis of their existing infrastructure, they were able to expand and gain economies of scale quickly. In many cases, the service concepts developed by these firms emphasized these advantages of scale, for example through the introduction of more standardized consulting 'products' (i.e. readily defined concepts that can be applied across large groups of clients). In addition, the consulting firms of this 'third wave' of the industry's development also differed from second-wave firms in terms of the topic areas on which they focused in their work. Many of their projects focused on the establishment of network structures, be they in the area of IT-based communication platforms or the creation of networks between suppliers and buyers along the value chain for particular products or services. Large third-wave firms not only advised their clients on how to design relationships, for example, between a firms and its outsourcing partners. Gradually, they would also become actively involved in such networks, e.g. as providers of outsourced services.

It would be wrong, however, to entirely equate the development of the third wave of the consulting industry with the establishment of consulting arms by the big IT and accounting firms. A range of smaller and more specialised consulting firms began to emerge, too, thereby increasing the supply of consulting services even further. Taking the German market as an example, a whole range of firms were founded in the 1980s on the back of their founders' strong capabilities in particular functional areas: Horváth & Partners (1981) in controlling, Simon Kucher & Partners (1984) in pricing and marketing, Droege & Comp. (1988) in cost reduction programmes, efficiency improvement and restructuring, and many others more. In addition, the consulting profession attracted many independent practitioners and small groups. Moreover, the borderline between consulting and other professional services – such as investment banking – became fuzzier, so that firms of either type began to enter the other's market space. Yet another source of increased supply was constituted by the establishment of in-house consulting units by many large 'client' firms. Some of these firms, such as Volkswagen's Gedas Group and Porsche Consulting, provide consulting services not only to their respective parent companies, but also to others, for example to suppliers and distributors in the wider network of their parent organisations.

Similar to what has happened on the demand side of the consulting market, the shifts on the supply side refer to changes with respect to both the *quantity* of supply and the *type* of services provided. Generally speaking, as service models mature, new types of players will enter the market with alternative service concepts, seeking to dethrone the established players. As we have seen above, this development has taken place in the consulting market before, with companies such as BCG and Bain in the 1960s and 1970s respectively pushing into the market for strategy consulting (followed later on by firms such as Monitor), a market that hitherto had been dominated by McKinsey & Company. The success of these firms can at least partly be attributed to the innovativeness of their service offerings. Similar developments have been taking place in recent years. The very fact that the consulting market is in the process of maturing and margins are declining invites young, innovative players to enter the market in order to attract the attention of clients. Large, established players are often barred by their very size from perceiving these new players as serious competitors.

Throughout the 1980s and the 1990s, the increasing supply in the consulting market was relatively easily soaked up by increased demand. For many years, the healthy conditions in the market provided the basis for above-average growth rates for many types of players, second- and third-wave firms alike. Similar to the internet and dotcom boom in the late 1990s, many of those involved believed that this expansion could last forever. The downturn in the capital markets in 2001, slower economic growth in that and the subsequent years, and the more uncertain political situation after September 11, 2001 let this belief falter almost over night. People began to realise that the consulting market was suddenly characterised by a phenomenon it had never known before, structural overcapacity.

2.3   The changing balance of power in the consulting market

The changes on the demand and the supply side of the consulting market do not relate merely to quantitative changes in the sense that lower prices would lead to the clearing of the market as supply outstrips demand. Of course, that development took place, too. Kennedy Information Services report that in 2003, for the first time in a long period, nominal prices for consulting services were stagnant, implying that real prices fell. However, if these quantitative changes were the only ones, they should decrease in importance as excess capacity was taken out of the market.

Yet, associated with the quantitative changes were qualitative developments that have tilted the nature of the relationships between consultants and clients in favour of the latter. In addition to the aspects discussed above, such as the availability of substitutes, two further factors provided clients with greater power vis-à-vis their consultants, relative to the situation during the boom years:

- *Greater choice*: As a result of the increase in the supply of consulting services in general, and the emergence of new types of consulting services in particular, clients are now in a far better position to 'pick and choose' the optimal service provider for a particular project they may want to undertake. Of course, consulting is still a relationship business. This does not imply, however, that consultants can sell any type of services on the back of existing client relationships. Today, clients can afford to be much more discerning in their choice of service providers. With better market information and easier access to evaluation tools such as rankings and surveys (as problematic as they may be), they can engage different consulting firms for different steps in the project value chain, or for different functional areas of expertise, more easily than used to be the case. They can also use meta-consultancies such as Cardea, based in Zurich, Switzerland, to fulfil this function on their behalf (Schmidt and Vogt, 2004). Whereas most projects in the 1980s were sold without a serious selection process guiding the choice of consultant, it is common nowadays to invite a whole range of advisors for 'pitch presentations' of the type known in the investment banking industry.

- *Increased experience and higher expectations*: Along the same lines, clients today are in a stronger bargaining position vis-à-vis their consultants, since the services provided by the latter have become a more mature offering. Whereas during the 1970s the presence of a consulting team in a company was still a fairly novel concept, today it is hard to find an organisation without a consulting firm being active in one or another part of the organisation. Today, except for projects of a more exotic nature, clients have a reasonably clear benchmark of what to expect from consultants. With many consultants having joined the ranks of their former clients, they also have an in-depth insight into the internal workings and processes of their consulting firms, including the basis for the calculation of their fees. In many cases, clients even involve their procurement departments in the selection of their consultants, and have fixed procedures for running the selection process. Overall, not only have clients higher expectations with respect to the performance of their advisors, they also have the means to ensure their expectations are met.

In sum, as a result of the developments discussed above, in addition to oversupply in the consulting market and restrained demand, the bargaining power of clients vis-à-vis their consultants has increased considerably in recent years. In the language of economics, the demand for consulting services has become much less inelastic than it used to be (Niewiem and Richter, 2004), implying that clients are less prepared to engage a consultant when the price offered appears unnecessarily high. In these situations, they are willing to put projects off, search for providers that offer better value for money, or find alternative solutions. These factors have worked in favour of clients, and put greater pressure on consultants. In an interview, one senior consultant reported that "these days, for every four weeks of project work, you need to do four weeks of bidding and negotiating beforehand".

In consequence, a greater share of the value added by consulting services accrues to clients. Consultants are left with lower margins, greater risks, and less value to satisfy the demands of their internal stakeholders.

3.   Organisational systems for competing in a changing market space

The discussion in the previous section has shown that the decrease in the margins available in the consulting market that took place between 2001 and 2003 is not just a temporary phenomenon. The upturn in the general economy should, of course, provide some breathing space to consulting firms, but it is unlikely that the conditions during the dotcom boom between 1995 and 2001 – or the general economic growth rates of the 1950s and 1960s – will return in the foreseeable future. Supply and demand conditions are such that margins in consulting, while still healthy as compared to other industries, will stay at significantly lower levels than was the case during the times of economic boom. Of course, there will always be firms that occupy niches, which offer more profitable business opportunities than others, but although the supply of such niches is not fixed, it is not unlimited, either. How will consulting firms cope with these changing conditions? How can they satisfy the demands of their internal stakeholders, and which organisational structures will help them to do so? In sections 3.1 and 3.2, I look in particular at the effects that the decrease in the value added that consulting firms can appropriate from their services will have on two key dimensions of their organisational systems: Their ownership and governance structures, and their organisational designs.

3.1   Ownership and governance

The majority of consulting firms are organised as partnerships. Figure 2, which analyses the 50 most prestigious consulting firms according to the Vault Report (Lerner, 2003) by ownership type, shows that 54 percent of these firms are owned and governed by a group of partners. 42 percent are wholly or partly owned by external investors, and even in these cases, senior employees often participate quite heavily in ownership.

Partnerships are defined as organisations in which a particular group of employees – usually senior members of the firm – share in two sets of interrelated rights:

- First, as the exclusive owners they are the recipients of the residual returns (whether positive or negative) generated by the firm's operations. In other words, once all legitimate claims of all other classes of patrons (suppliers, buyers, financiers, non-owner employees) are satisfied, the partners receive what is left over of the firm's cash flow. In some years, these residual returns can be unusually high. On the other hand, they serve as a risk premium for those years in which the claims of those classes of patrons who are not owners exceed the firm's revenues. In other words, in partnerships profits are distributed and risks are borne by insiders, rather than by others outside the firm.

Ownership of Leading Consulting Firms

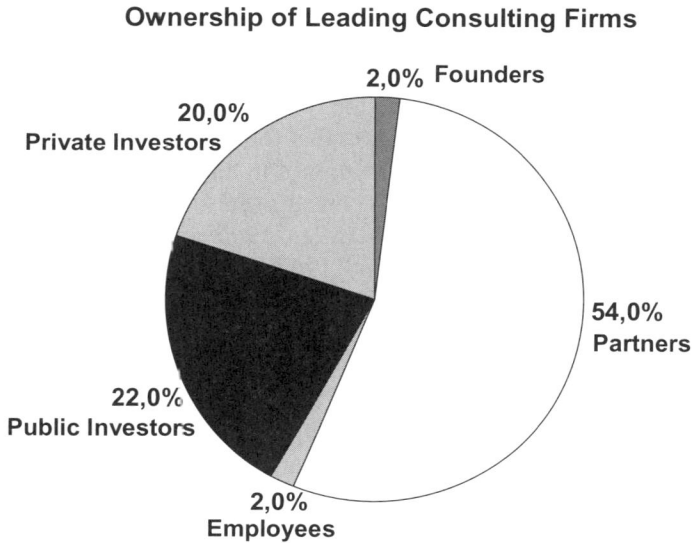

Fig. 2. The 50 most reputable consulting firms according to the Vault Report (Lerner, 2003) by ownership type

Classes of Patrons in Consulting Firms

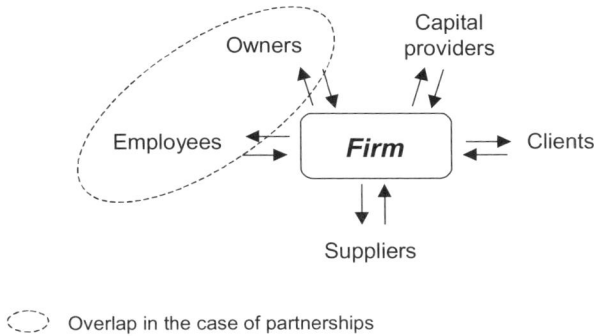

Fig. 3. Classes of patrons in consulting firms

- Second, the partners in professional service firms hold the exclusive governance rights over their organisations. Not only do they receive the profits of the firm, they also decide on their use, as well as on other managerial issues. Therefore, partnerships are not characterised by the 'division of ownership and control' which Berle and Means (1991; originally published in 1932) analysed to be the root cause of the corporate governance conflicts in many large firms usually owned by external shareholders. In partnerships, a group of the senior employees fulfils both the roles of managers and owners. Consequently, in most partnerships the differentiation between operating and administrative functions is very limited.

From an economics point of view, partnerships serve a dual purpose (Milgrom and Roberts 1992, pp. 522-524). First, they facilitate bonding among the partners. In this context, 'bonding' primarily means that partners post a bond, i.e. a guarantee, of the firm's good behaviour and professional competence. In a pure partnership model, the partners' potential liabilities are unlimited, hence if the firm does poor quality work or engages in illegal practices, claimants can go after the partners' personal assets. In this sense, the partners 'bond' one another. Although many firms have moved away from legal structures in which the partners carry full unlimited liability (e.g. with the introduction of limited liability partnerships), it is still the case that in partnerships the partners bear at least some responsibility for the quality of each others' work, not only their own. In addition, the expression 'bonding' has a socio-psychological connotation. Partnerships provide scope for shared socialisation, the development of a common culture, and for mutual understanding.

Second, and in connection with the bonding argument, they allow partners to monitor each other (and the rest of the firm), as partners develop an understanding of each other's activity. Partners will post a bond only if they can assess the quality of each others' activity, hence bonding requires monitoring.

While a partnership facilitates the development of bonding and monitoring, it also requires these factors for its stability. If, for example, the ability of partners to observe and assess each other's work decreases (e.g. due to increased heterogeneity among the partnership group), some partners may deliver sub-optimal performance. As a result, the partnership structure will become a less efficient governance system for the firm concerned.

In recent years, we have seen a movement away from the use of partnership governance. Several stock-market listed companies began to establish consulting operations, or to acquire them. In other cases, consulting firms decided to go public of their own accord. While there were some exceptions to this trend – most notably the management buy-out of Roland Berger Strategy Consultants from Deutsche Bank in 1998 in order to re-establish their earlier partnership structure – big, integrated consulting firms in particular chose to abandon their status as partnerships in order to limit their liabilities, and to gain access to external capital needed for expansion.

3.2   Organisational design

As a result of the increased competition and the reduced margins in the consulting market, the pressure on the players in this market to reduce their costs and build efficient administrative structures increases significantly. This pressure works on two levels: First, it forces consulting firms across the board to realise efficiency gains. In recent years, even the most prestigious firms have made significant efforts to slash costs and develop leaner structures. Second, it reinforces a trend in the consulting market which has been apparent before, namely the growing bifurcation between firms organised along the professional partnership (P2) model and those that can be characterised as managed professional businesses (MPBs).

The P2 model was the dominant organisational form of those consulting firms that developed during the 'second wave' of the industry's evolution, which took place between the 1950s and the 1970s (see figure 2 above). The use of the partnership model – in terms of the ownership model as discussed above and in terms of the professional ethic and identity of these firms – during this period was so prevalent that Greenwood, Hinings, and Brown (1990) describe the firms as adhering to the professional partnership *archetype*.

In the further evolution of the consulting industry, as the focus of clients shifted to a greater emphasis on implementation issues, to IT-related services, and to services of a more operational nature, a new type of consulting firm emerged. Companies that provide these types of services often have greater capital requirements than firms providing 'pure' consulting services in the sense of high-level advice to top management. Their internal administration is in the hands of a smaller group of managers with limited or no client contact, as compared to the more distributed management function found in P2-type firms. Cooper, Hinings,

Greenwood and Brown (1996) describe this model as the managed professional business (MPB) archetype.

In addition to matters of ownership arrangements and governance systems, P2- and MPB-type firms tend to differ with respect to critical aspects of their organisational designs. These aspects include:

- *Leverage ratio*: In P2-type firms, teams tend to be smaller, so that junior consultants work closely with their senior colleagues (e.g. partners) and thus receive a lot of 'airtime'. The classical model of human resource development in P2-type firms is that of the apprenticeship, where junior consultants learn through direct cooperation with senior 'master' consultants. In MPB-type firms, teams tend to be larger, as junior consultants carry out their activities according to more clearly pre-defined working schedules. As a result, the leverage ratio (Maister 1993) in these firms – the average number of junior consultants per senior consultant – tends to be larger than in P2-type firms.

- *Performance assessment systems*: Many P2-type firms use promotion systems which labour economists would characterise as tournaments, i.e. as relative performance assessment systems with risk. In other words, the performance of individual consultants at a given seniority level is assessed relative to the performance of their respective peer group, and individuals who fare badly in this comparison are asked to leave the firm. As a result, the average tenure of consultants in P2-type firms is low, as compared to many MPB-type firms. In the latter group, employees are often allowed to stay on a given seniority level for a longer period of time, leading to greater stability of the workforce (from the perspective of the firm) and a less pressurised work environment (from the perspective of employees).

- *Differentiation between administrative functions and service provision*: As mentioned above, MPB-type firms tend to be characterised by a greater differentiation between employees involved in the provision of consulting (or other client-facing) services, and units dedicated to providing administrative activities in support of the organisation as such. In contrast, in P2-type firms it is not unusual for senior consultants (e.g. partners) to bear ultimate responsibility for administrative functions such as human resources (HR) management, finance, and so on. Even consultants below partner level are expected to become involved in 'internal' services to the firm, e.g. the organisation of events, involvement in recruitment activities, and so on. As an example, in the prototypical P2-type firms, the HR department has only little involvement with the selection and hiring of new consultants, except for the organisation and facilitation of the process. Interviews with applicants are generally conducted by experienced consultants at project manager level or above, and hiring decisions are taken by partners. In contrast, in MPB-type firms, the intake of new recruits is often so large that human resource specialists simply have to take a more prominent role in the recruitment process. Senior consultants may still take the hiring decisions, but the processes leading to such decisions are less unilaterally driven by them.

3.3   Alternative systems of consulting firms

Sections 3.1 and 3.2 described the differences between P2- and MPB-type consulting firms, using their differences with respect to governance systems and organisational structures as examples. In this section, the argument is taken a step further. I propose that the P2- and MPB-archetypes represent two fundamentally different organisational systems that consulting firms can adopt. Each of these two systems consists of (and relies for its operation on) a number of elements that are complementary to each other. The word 'complementarity' is used here in an economic sense. "Several activities are mutually complementary if doing more of any one activity increases (or at least does not decrease) the marginal profitability of each other activity in the group" (Milgrom and Roberts 1992, p. 108). If one or more of the elements on which the system relies is taken away, the stability of the entire system is endangered. One of the conditions for the stability of the P2-system of consulting firms consists of high rents, i.e. the ability of the firms concerned to appropriate a significant part of the value generated by their services. Hence, the eroding margins in the consulting industry tend to destabilise the P2-system, in particular with respect to the weaker firms.

More specifically, the P2-system of consulting firms relies for its stability on at least the following four factors: Partnership governance, a professional orientation, a single business focus, and high rents.

System 1: The P2-Model

Partnership governance	Professional orientation
Single business focus	High rents

Fig. 4. System 1: The P2-model

In order to illustrate the complementarity between the four elements in this model, consider the relationship between partnership governance and professional orientation. Partnerships are not characterised merely by the allocation of ownership rights to a particular class of patrons, but also by a particular working ethic, understood in a broad sense. Many partnerships see themselves not as businesses aimed at profit maximisation, but as professional practices whose primary objective is to serve their clients. Profits follow adherence to the professional approach; they are not the initial objective.

Admittedly, this description of partnerships is broad-brush and oversimplifying: One can find examples of consulting firms owned by partners that do not share these professional ideals, as well as consulting firms owned by external investors that do. Nevertheless, assuming ownership rights can help senior employees develop a sense of identity with their firm, of equality with their partners, and of personal responsibility and professional independence from outside influences. Thereby, partnership in the sense of an ownership arrangement can contribute to the development of the 'spirit' of partnership.

Similar arguments can be developed with respect to the relationship between partnership governance and a single business focus. Partnerships rely for their stability on the ability of the partners to work together closely, and to ensure that each of the partners makes an adequate performance contribution. Only if the quality of the partners' work is ensured, will a firm be able to charge prices that provide it with superior rents. Diversification renders mutual monitoring more difficult. Therefore, diversification strategies are almost automatically combined with the need to establish organisational structures and management systems that cover both the consulting arm and the other business activity, whatever it may consist of. Hence, the professional partnership model requires a single-mindedness that diversified firms often have a hard time emulating. Diversified firms typically do not flourish if structured as professional partnerships, nor have we seen many professional partnerships prosper if they run diversified businesses.

Finally, and critically, substantial rents complement other elements of the P2 model. High profitability gives a firm a degree of independence, allowing the partners to refuse assignments that might detract from the firm's chosen focus or compromise the professional ethic. Large and growing profits increase the likelihood of cooperation that is central to partnership governance. There will be fewer squabbles over division of the pie when the pie itself grows year on year.

The second system that consulting firms can adopt relates to the MPB-model, crucial aspects of which were already discussed above. Again, at least four mutually complementary elements of this system can be identified.

System 2: The MPB-Model

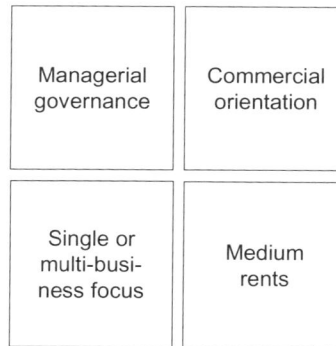

Managerial governance	Commercial orientation
Single or multi-business focus	Medium rents

Fig. 5. System 2: The MPB-model

Consultants working in MPB-type firms can (and should!) adopt a more commercially minded perspective on their work. This has nothing to do with unethical behaviour. In order to provide consulting services at reasonable costs, MPB-type firms are in particular need to control their cost structures, and to develop efficient infrastructures. These infrastructures can serve as a good basis for diversification, since different (related) lines of business can share in a common administrative set-up. These are just a few examples for the many complementarities among the different elements in the MPB-model.

Having analysed P2- and MPB-type consulting firms, the critical question is whether the trend (however slow) away from the use of partnership structures is reflective of many consulting firms' weakened capacity to appropriate a fair share of the value generated by their services. Although it may be too early to answer this question conclusively, indications are that this is so (Graubner and Richter, 2003). Partnerships rely for their operations on the ability of senior employees to extract value added from their services so they are prepared to accept the risks and disadvantages associated with ownership. Partnerships can only work if the partners are able and willing to

- provide sufficient capital for their firm – both for its current operations and for its future growth plans
- contribute to the governance of the firm at low cost
- make personal sacrifices in times of economic difficulties

Individuals will only invest in attaining or maintaining partnership status if they expect the benefits to exceed the costs and risks involved in doing so. If the risks rise, and the benefits decrease, fewer people will make these investments. For example, with reduced enthusiasm for the final reward (partnership), they may not work as hard during the years before being elected partners, as previous generations of consultants would have done. Existing partners may contribute less to the governance of the firm, focusing instead on quick revenue generation. Doing so may be beneficial to them in the short term, but detrimental to the management of their respective firm in the longer run. They may also be more cautious in providing capital to the firm, if and when it needs it, as they may perceive the risks involved as being too high. This problem is particularly relevant for those consulting firms whose business model requires significant investment into infrastructure, e.g. for firms involved in IT consulting or outsourcing.

In sum, the increase in the risk-reward-ratio induced by the changing market environment can be expected to have adverse effects on the economic stability of partnerships in the longer run. If this hypothesis is correct, we should expect more firms to move away from partnership structures, e.g. by issuing shares on the stock market, or by divesting themselves to other companies or private investors. Of course, should a significant number of firms in fact move away from the use of partnership, those that remain partnerships will capitalise on the increased distinctiveness of their ownership and governance structure.

3.4   The bifurcation in the consulting market

In the above section, the contrast between the organisational designs of P2- and MPB-type firms was painted in stronger colours than may be warranted in reality. Many consulting companies continue to fall in between these two ends of the spectrum. However, as the margins in the consulting markets become narrower and the pressure to define a unique strategic position stronger, the bifurcation between the two systems should increase. Companies that are 'stuck in the middle' of the two extremes will have to redefine their position, or risk coming under pressure by competitors from both sides. They will find that the high ground of the classical P2-type players is thoroughly covered by the existing brands, leaving little room for any but a few small firms. With intense competition in the top segment of the consulting market, and only moderate growth prospects, it is hard to see how further companies can break into the ring of the top-tier players.

The alternative route for the larger second and third tier players is to give up the fight for the high ground, and re-position themselves as consultants with a more operational outlook. That business model is not to be frowned upon. It allows the firms that use it to provide important services that the P2-type firms would have a hard time doing – take the example of the IT integration following acquisitions, which requires the ability to carry out projects with hundreds of people involved.

Several factors, two of which I will discuss in the following, push second tier players to establish themselves as managed professional businesses. First, as the pressure to contain costs increases in the consulting market, the importance of scale and the savings associated with it increases, too. It has long been known that in consulting firms the work of junior consultants helps to finance the senior professionals (see the chapter by Tom Sommerlatte in this book). Therefore, in order to secure their profitability under increased pressure, many consulting firms tend to increase their leverage, hiring juniors without a corresponding increase at the senior levels of the hierarchy. In doing so, they inadvertently change the nature of the services they provide: Their services become more operational in nature, i.e. they use more closely specified procedures, project plans and so on, in order to enable these junior consultants to function with limited supervision from senior professionals. Of course, it is possible to stay with the professional partnership model and still grow – but that requires all levels of the organisation to grow concomitantly at roughly the same speed.

Second, increased competition in the consulting market implies that the weaker firms look for mechanisms – whether rational or not – to protect themselves from the risk of failure. A classical strategy in the tool box for protection consists of diversification. Years before the risk of failure becomes publicly apparent, firms may resort to acquisitions that lead them away from their core competency, or venture into businesses that are only indirectly related to consulting. This strategy may well be successful, and it is not to be sneered upon. However, as argued above, diversification is not easily compatible with the professional partnership model.

Phrased differently, the argument developed in the above section can be summarised as follows. The stability of the professional partnership model in consulting firms relies on the capacity of these firms, respectively the people working in them, to extract rents from the services provided for the purposes of the firms as such. If that capacity is reduced, as is currently happening, then fewer firms can organise themselves in this way. They will look for alternative organisational models, or move into different business segments. As a result, the market bifurcates. How big the circle of those firms that can retain their professional partnership structures will be, is yet unclear.

It would also take gazing into the crystal ball to answer the question of whether the model of managed professional business firms is viable in the long run, or whether entirely new models of consulting firms may emerge. Since the mid-1990s, we have seen a new generation of network-based firms emerge which capitalise on their ability to tailor consulting services to the specific needs of clients, and cooperate with a whole range of partner firms so as to leverage their skills in an optimal way. Of course, the stability of these network-based firms is still to be proven, yet it might well be that the bifurcation in the market described above may only be the first step towards a much more far-reaching trend towards *fragmentation*. What is clear, however, is that the changing dynamics of the consulting market has a fundamental impact on the strategies and structures of consulting firms.

References

Berle, Adolf A./Means, Gardiner C. (1991): The Modern Corporation and Private Property, Transaction Publishers, New Brunswick, New Jersey.

Cooper, David J./Hinings, Bob/Greenwood, Royston/Brown, John L. (1996): Sedimentation and Transformation in Organizational Change: The Case of Canadian Law Firms, in: Organization Studies, Vol. 17, No. 4, pp. 623-647.

Graubner, Michael/Richter, Ansgar (2003): Managing Tomorrow's Consulting Firm, in: Consulting to Management, Vol. 14, No. 3, 2003, pp. 43-50.

Greenwood, Royston/Hinings, Bob/Brown, John L. (1990): "P2-form" Strategic Management: Corporate Practices in Professional Partnerships, in: Academy of Management Journal, Vol. 33, No. 4, 1990, pp. 725-755.

Henderson, James/Boscheck, Ralf (1991): Competition in the European Management Consulting Industry, 1990, IMD Case 395-009-5, 1991.

Kahn, Ely J. (1986): The Problem Solvers: A History of Arthur D. Little, Inc. Little, Brown & Company: Boston, Toronto.

Kipping, Matthias (2002): Trapped in Their Wave: The Evolution of Management Consultancies, in: Clark, Timothy/Fincham, Robin (eds.): Critical Consulting. New Perspectives on the Management Advice Industry, Blackwell Publishers, Oxford/Malden (Mass.), pp. 28-49.

Lerner, Marcy (2003): Vault Guide to the Top 50 Management and Strategy Consulting Firms, Vault Inc, New York.

Maister, David H. (1993): Managing the Professional Service Firm,. Free Press,: New York et al.

Milgrom, Paul/Roberts, John (1992): Economics, Organization and Management, Prentice-Hall Englewood Cliffs, NJ.

Niewiem, Sandra/Richter, Ansgar (2004): The Changing Balance of Power in the Consulting Market, in: Business Strategy Review, Vol. 15, No. 1, 2004, pp. 8-13.

Schmidt, Sascha L./Vogt, Patrick (2004): Emergence of New Business Models in Strategy Consulting, in: Academy of Management Conference Proceedings, 2nd International Conference on Management Consulting, Lausanne, pp. 137-143.

Wittreich, Warren J. (1966): How to Buy / Sell Professional Services, in: Harvard Business Review, March-April 1966, pp. 127-136.

PART III

THE DEVELOPMENT OF THE CONSULTING INDUSTRY

Life Cycle Phenomena in the Consulting Sector – Driving Forces of Fundamental Value Changes

Tom Sommerlatte

1. From craftsmanship to a maturing industry

When formulating the title of this paper, I resisted the temptation to use the term consulting "industry" although consulting has accumulated a number of traits of a maturing industry.

With estimated worldwide revenues of $180 billion annually (management consulting, IT-consulting and human resource consulting combined) and about 1.5 million professional consultants worldwide, with several global consulting firms in the size category of 10,000 to 100,000 people, consulting does indeed show industry characteristics, including growing standardization of service products, economy of scale effects, market saturation in many of the service product areas, price and margin pressure, restructuring and so on.

For someone like myself who chose a career in consulting (in the 1970s) when it was a profession with a lot of individualism, craftsmanship and pioneering personalities and firms, it has been an overwhelming change – but one that our success itself has engendered.

As often when industries progress in their life cycle, some participants – often the larger ones – are reluctant to admit and accept change as it affects established positions, styles and economics.

What a change for a top management consultant to have to negotiate a reduction of billing rates with the purchasing department of his client's organisation! What a different relationship when the client contact has previously been a consultant himself, or when the client company avails of its own group of smart in house consultants! What a new situation when companies invite ten or more hungry consulting firms to submit a proposal and compete for a project, and subsequently take part in a 'beauty contest' in front of a committee of more or less anonymous decision-makers!

But change will continue and will put the laggards increasingly at odds with reality.

Therefore, it is essential to be aware of the driving forces of change, the new business dynamics and the choices and opportunities that consulting firms have to face.

2.   What are the driving forces of change?

While in the earlier life cycle phases of consulting (embryonic, pioneering, early growth, fast growth) the challenge for consultants was to prove they could be useful and they were able to penetrate "virgin" clients, once the penetration had progressed, the challenge shifted to value and brand differentiation and economies of scale.

Much of the earlier success of a consulting firm was indeed due to its ability to convince decision makers (mostly at top management level) that using a consultant could help and was not a sign of weakness, and also due to its ability to create awareness of and acceptance for its consulting services, and to build trust and exclusive relationships.

In an increasingly crowded and competitive environment, in which nearly all client companies have past or on-going experience with consultants and in which consulting services are well proven and increasingly similar across a wide range of providers, the success of a consulting firm is a function of its ability to create a differentiated reputation and to compete on the basis of proven experience/references, cost-effective approaches, and the availability of well orchestrated consulting teams.

In their struggle for profitability, productivity, growth or survival, most client companies are today proactively calling on consultants and going after established consulting service products. But they are also aware that they can be highly selective and demanding because of more or less pronounced overcapacity in the consulting sector. Therefore, they "shop around" and exert pressure on prices.

Along with these changes in market conditions, the value that consultants are expected to provide has changed as well.

While in the pioneering and growth phases, the main value of consultants was their ability to take a "helicopter view" of a company's situation in order to help overcome established thinking and operating routines and apply a more creative way of dealing with strategic issues, the current leading service products are the implementation of something already decided, rationalizing business processes by integrating them into the IT-based enterprise system, and streamlining operational systems.

Even though general economic conditions and the maturing of most industry sectors – including some of the long-standing growth sectors such as the IT and the telecommunications industry – continue to call for rationalization, these consulting service products are themselves reaching saturation in the market.

As the global economy will swing back to higher GNP rates sooner or later and new growth opportunities for consulting will emerge, it is important to understand the business dynamics of the consulting sector and to prepare for future value changes.

3. What are the business dynamics?

In large and mature industries, growth is not absent, but it is taking place in selected sub-sectors to the detriment of other sub-sectors. Similarly, in the consulting market there have been, are and will be sub-sectors responding to growing demand while other sub-sectors will be losing out.

One way of segmenting the consulting market is, of course, by client industry. And, indeed, there have recently been substantial shifts within the stagnant overall consulting market: financial industries, the IT, telecommunications and media industries have sharply reduced their consulting intake, while the public sector, utilities, the healthcare and the transportation industries have increased their demand.

To focus primarily on growth sectors can, however, represent a strategic disadvantage. In order to develop an industry positioning, a consulting firm has to build up industry knowledge and industry-experienced staff and has then to deal with the ups and downs of the chosen industries.

More importantly, the mix of demand for consulting services in a given industry follows cross-industry patterns, often stimulated by consulting firms emphasizing and investing in the development and marketing of general service products. Once a new service product begins to raise interest, this will spread over most industry sectors, leaving the established industry consultants in a position of "old hat".

Therefore, in the rapidly changing environment of the consulting sector, the decisive business dynamics are those of service product life cycles. Many of the existing service products have already fully penetrated the market. In order to grow, consulting firms that have gained their position and reputation with these have to be able to transfer their skills and their image to new, growing service product areas forcefully.

But these new service product areas also offer smaller or new consulting firms the opportunity to grow with them and, therefore, more rapidly than the overall consulting market.

It is therefore crucial to understand early on, which strategic and operational concerns, priorities and directions show promise of being recognized by the business community as the most pertinent ones.

Certain people claim that consultants make up themes and "hot buttons" through publications and promotional campaigns in order to create new consulting turfs. To believe this, implies that the business community can be talked into "fads" and into spending large amounts on more or less useless consulting advice.

It is much more realistic to assume a match between growing management needs under evolving market, competitive and technological pressures on the one hand and a way of articulating these needs and offering a new approach to dealing with them on the other hand.

Consulting firms that home in on this evolving match early on, that work intensively at exploring appropriate problem-solving approaches and manage to associate reputation and credibility with a new subject area, stand a good chance of growing with this new area.

Not every newly emerging area of need is, of course, long-lived and sizable. But those areas that are increasingly perceived as having a strong impact on competitiveness and/or business potential will become burning ones for a rapidly growing number of executives. They represent fertile hunting ground for those consulting firms that have credibly associated themselves with the issue area at hand and are believed to offer effective remedies.

4.   We are experiencing another transition

However, there are major constraints, which limit the growth potential of consulting. Client companies have increasingly learnt how to tackle issue areas themselves, they have become demanding with respect to the credentials of consultants, and they have now developed the habit of bargaining for the lowest consulting cost.

Fink et. al. (2004) have been able to show that it is the client perception of a consulting firm's credentials in a given service product area that plays a key role in the decision to hire the firm or not. The experience of many client companies with consultants and the results obtained have been disappointing, or at least sobering. Most companies have therefore adopted a restrictive perception of where and to what extent they can trust consultants, correlating names of consulting firms with specific service product areas, specific capabilities, types of people and operating styles.

This is propitious for established consulting firms in their established service product areas, but it is a threat when established consulting products no longer generate growth and new products are become increasingly important.

We are currently experiencing such a transition.

There is a growing need to use IT and communication systems for more than process reengineering and cost cutting, and to add value by more than restructuring companies and industries. The name of the game is to explore new growth opportunities, to innovate product and service offerings, to move away from mere price competition and to deploy human resources and their intellectual capabilities in more effective ways.

Top management of many client companies is sensing this need but, in most cases, does not yet dare to forcefully take new initiatives in this direction. In the last few years of economic downturn, anything smelling of risk, investment in future businesses or incurring avoidable costs has been out of the question. In mature industries, cost competitiveness and transferring production to low-cost countries have by far been the dominant preoccupation.

However, while consulting service products such as business process reengineering, total quality management, lean management and delayering/downsizing are themselves maturing, customer relationship management, knowledge management, technology and innovation management and e-business strategies are increasingly being explored in pioneering companies (Sommerlatte 2001).

Whether they will move from the speculative and explorative phase to full-flung market penetration will depend on how credible the performance and value reasoning for these new thrusts can be made.

Academia, management literature, top executive preferences and business development efforts of consulting firms will determine which of the thrusts will become the next growth segments for the consulting sector.

And a lot will depend on which consulting firms will be able to establish and justify a leadership position in these new areas.

5. Which consulting firms can gain credibility for the new value propositions?

Established consulting firms have either consciously built or simply accumulated a reputation for the type of consulting work for which they can be trusted.

Client companies tend to consider this reputation as an indicator of the mindset and type of people and approach that they can expect from the consulting firm. This reputation is not easily transferable to other consulting product areas and can be a major obstacle when considering services from a given consulting firm in other areas.

In their research, based on a survey at about 240 German companies, Fink et. al. (2004) found that executives do indeed have an entrenched perception of the service products that consulting firms are strong or not so strong in.

Name some of the leading consulting firms and off hand you will be able to say which of them are associated strongly with business process reengineering, lean management or shareholder value optimisation, implying that they will typically be called in when cost cutting and streamlining are the issues at hand. Similarly, when strategy development is asked for, a different set of reputed consulting firms comes to mind, implying that they have a systematic and effective approach to thinking creatively or pragmatically about business options.

But how about customer relationship management, knowledge management, technology and innovation management or e-business-strategies – the fast paced consulting service product areas?

Can the established consulting firms effectively transfer credibility from their entrenched positions in business process reengineering, total quality management, lean management or strategy consulting to the growing consulting areas such as customer relationship management, knowledge management, innovation management and e-business? Will client companies be prepared to hire what they consider restructuring experts or strategy analysts to help them transform their company into an innovation-driven knowledge-based organisation?

Or will new consulting firms conquer these new areas and offer new value, just as IT-consulting firms emerged and outgrew many of the established consulting firms at the time when client companies began to increasingly look to IT-based enterprise systems?

6. Will the consulting sector overcome its symptoms of maturing?

Just as in any other industry, in the consulting sector, too, market saturation, overcapacity, diminishing differentiation and shrinking margins have led to continued reduced investment in product development.

As long as overcapacity, lack of differentiation and price erosion continue to exist, the symptoms of a maturing industry will prevail in the consulting sector – also to the disadvantage of its clients.

A look at the typical cost structures of a consulting firm shows why this is the case. Table 1 is an example of a strategy consulting firm and shows the typical mid-range case of a consultant, a manager and a director with an underlying staff pyramid of two managers per Partner and three consultants per manager.

Salary and bonus levels are not negotiable if consulting firms want to attract top people (which is to a large extent their raison d'être). All other cost items shown are essential for doing business and have to be included in the billing rates.

The main variable is, therefore, the number of chargeable days, which determines the theoretical billing rate per day needed to cover cost and a minimum profit contribution.

Out of 225 available working days per year (weekends, holidays and an average number of sick days excluded), a consultant typically spends about 50 days per year on work for lost proposals, internal purposes and training, while managers and partners have to invest in the order of 100 days each in business development, client relationship management, marketing, staff development/training, product development, proposal preparation, presentation and negotiation. Partners spend an additional 25 days per year on leading practices and managing the firm.

On the basis of the staff pyramid described earlier, the total cost and profit contribution of such a pyramid (one partner, two managers, six consultants) adds up to over 2 million Euros per year. In order to generate the necessary contract volume, and assuming that one out of three proposals is successful, proposals to the tune of 6.0 million Euros have to be prepared and submitted. At a contract size of 500,000 Euros, the number of proposals submitted would, therefore, be 12, and the number of clients to be courted in the order of 20 to 30 (hence the high number of non-chargeable days of partners and managers).

At the billing rates that can be realized in the market under "normal conditions", partners and managers contribute little to no profit, the entire profit contribution being generated by the consultants. The value of their work, however, depends largely on the quality of thought and the leadership of the partners and managers.

Example of mid-of-the-range cost structures in a strategy consulting firm

Item	Consultant (Euro/Year)	Manager (Euro/Year)	Partner (Euro/Year)
Salary	60.000	100.000	200.000
Social costs, retirement programme, health insurance	15.000	24.000	45.000
Shared costs, secretarial, space, administration	20.000	40.000	80.000
IT & telecom equipment	9.000	17.000	20.000
Depreciation & operating costs			
Non-chargeable travel costs	5.000	20.000	40.000
Training expenses	5.000	-	-
Material, literature, PR	6.000	9.000	15.000
Bonus (variable)	10.000	40.000	80.000
Profit contribution (20 %)	25.000	50.000	100.000
Total	**155.000**	**300.000**	**580.000**
Number of chargeable days	175	125	100
Theoretical billing rate	900	2.400	5.800
Market-based billing rate	1.000	2.000	5.000
Revenues	175.000	250.000	500.000

Table 1. Example of-mid-of-the-range cost structures in a strategy consulting firm

At the margin pressure we are currently observing in the consulting business, the economics of this business are severely endangered:

- Client companies inviting more and more competitors to propose on RFPs causes the ratio of contracts obtained to the proposals submitted to shrink, thus increasing the non-chargeable time of partners and managers and leading to even higher cost undercoverage on their part.

- Billing rates being negotiated downwards, especially those of consultants, reduces their contribution per chargeable day and forces consulting firms to extract more days out of their consultants – at the expense of training, weekends and holidays – and ultimately at the expense of the consultants' willingness to stay with the firm.

- Growing pressure on margins forces consulting firms to cut down on product development in favour of increased standardization, and to neglect research into new business issues and the pioneering of new solutions. Thus, the lack of differentiation and innovation, typical of maturing industries is enhanced – and further margin pressure is the result.

Will the consulting sector be able to overcome its symptoms of a maturing industry and see new, substantial growth?

The potential is certainly there since almost all industry sectors are in growing need of new business models and opportunities. The challenge for the consulting firms is to resist cutting short on issue research, service product development and staff training, and to continue to attract the best, i.e. the most creative, dedicated and ambitious candidates, and to differentiate themselves in terms of culture, style and positioning.

References

Fink Dietmar/Knoblach Bianka (2004): Strategische Planung in der Unternehmensberatung, in: Sommerlatte Tom/Mirow Michael/Niedereichholz Christel/ von Windau, Peter (eds.): Handbuch der Unternehmensberatung. Organisationen führen und entwickeln, Erich Schmidt Verlag, Berlin, ch. 7310.

Sommerlatte Tom (2001): Strategie, Innovation, Kosteneffizienz, Symposion Publishing, Düsseldorf.

The Role of Governance and Values in the Consulting Industry

Klaus-Peter Gushurst and Joachim Deinlein

1. Introduction

The consulting industry is facing a period of unprecedented change. Whereas for many years the sector consistently enjoyed growth rates of around 15 % to 20 % p.a., more recently there has been a downturn in growth and only now are we beginning to see a renewed turnup in demand from corporate clients. The forecast for the coming years is for only a modest increase in the rate of growth, something which has not been experienced in the sector since the early 1980s. This in itself is set to have an impact on the sector as a whole and on the need of consulting firms to "refresh" or adjust their strategies.

At the same time, several other structural changes are significantly changing the face of the industry. Following the 'boom period', which accompanied the rise of the New Economy, the consulting sector is currently going through a period where consolidations, takeovers and mergers are the driving forces in the sector. Accounting firms, which had to get rid of their consulting arms, are silently building up management consulting services again. Given that the economy as a whole has been experiencing a shake-up, we have also seen changing buying patterns on behalf of the clients (e.g. "preferred supplier arrangements"), with knock-on effects, in particular for the structure of the consulting sector.

This chapter will give a short overview of the current market challenges consulting firms are facing. In particular, we look at the implications for corporate governance in the wake of the spectacular corporate collapses and scandals in 2001 and 2002. In the light of this new commercial environment, we consider the advantage which independent partnerships and ownership structures enjoy in terms of their governance mechanisms.

Following this analysis we investigate in greater detail the need for a values-driven agenda to support the corporate governance mechanisms, as well as the consequences of this need both for corporate managers in general and for those working in the consulting field in particular. We develop a perspective as to how governance systems, and especially values, help to steer companies through the changes, taking the Booz Allen Hamilton approach as a specific example.

2. Current challenges in consulting, and critical success factors going forward

An initial observation is that there are a number of factors which continue to foster a mood of caution in the wider economy – economic growth in the EU is sluggish, and in the case of Germany the implementation of structural reforms to the economy is partially being held up. High unemployment persists in Germany and in several other EU states, while interest rates are proving volatile and are moving upwards once again. The continuing uncertainty generated by the war on terrorism, and by terrorist acts themselves, is also serving as a brake on entrepreneurial activity.

Nevertheless, the present economic context is one of cautious optimism going forward, and can be attributed to a number of factors. Business sentiment is improving, and we are seeing private equity investors gradually returning to the market. The S&P 500 is up nearly 200 % this year, and there has been a revival in the global IPO market. Within this context, the strategy consulting industry as a whole is gradually regaining momentum, and the prediction is for a return to growth over the coming years (see figure 1).

**Strategy Consulting Industry –
Market Size and Annual Growth Rates**

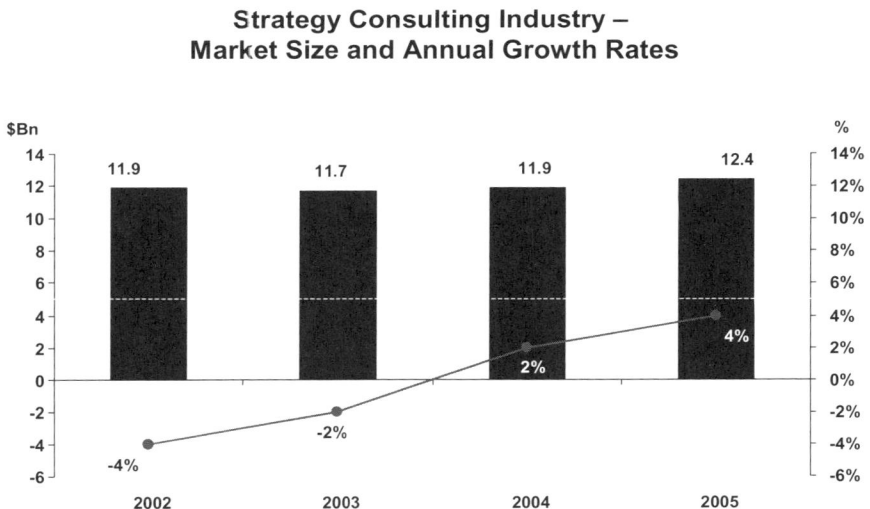

Fig. 1. Strategy Consulting Industry (Source: Czerniawska/Lyons, 2003, p. 45)

However, the projected growth is of modest proportions, and a Financial Times survey in April 2003 revealed that "none of the [39] consulting firms questioned believed that a substantial recovery is on the horizon" (Parker, 2003, p. 5); moreover, it comes in the wake of what The Economist described as an "annus horribilis for strategy consultants". The projected levels of growth are well below what has historically been the case, and this is generating pressure for far-reaching structural change within the sector.

2.1 Turbulent times for consultants

What are the particular elements creating such a turbulent climate for the consulting sector? We would highlight three mega-trends:

1. **Overcapacity and consolidation:** Having experienced a significant acceleration in expansion during the period of the New Economy, the recent reversals in this area and the broader economic slowdown are now resulting in overcapacity in the consulting sector. We are seeing a massive reduction in the number of players and firms, with a polarisation of the industry based on size (scale) and internationalisation (worldwide presence). The middle ground for consulting companies is being eroded, and the options are increasingly to move towards operating on a global scale, or to develop specialisation in niche markets for consulting activity (i.e. spin-offs), and to "cherry-pick", very often on functional issues.

2. **Changes in purchasing behaviour:** There has been a reduction in the supplier base, with preferred-supplier approaches being increasingly used. Framework contracts are more frequently being applied to consulting, and the principle of pay-per-performance is gaining ground. The knock-on effect is a shift away from the traditional role of the consultant, which was largely to carry out an analysis and make strategic recommendations. The work of today's consultant is more towards "results-driven" coaching, capability transfer, and supporting clients as they execute strategic transformations.

3. **Increased client expectations:** Time frames are becoming increasingly tight, with a demand for short-term solutions with rapid payback. Clients are demanding in-depth expertise and the involvement of senior consultants, very often they are looking for global servicing across strategy, operations and technical issues.

These pressures will combine with lower sectoral growth over the next few years to increase the challenges for consulting companies. Structured purchasing and framework contracts for general management consulting companies are leading to increased competition, and pay per performance is increasing the pressure for discernible payback in shorter time frames. The implications of this are that virtually all general management consulting firms are engaged in a fight to secure new work, and are required to display new capabilities in Operations, IT and Change Management, or to diversify into other growing segments of the business, e.g. the public sector. Accordingly, we are seeing increased differentiation among consulting companies.

Despite the forecasted return to growth outlined above, it should again be emphasised that this is at a level for the sector last experienced during the 1980s, and this calls all current consulting business models into question. The models are essentially predicated on a pyramid-like structure, with high growth delivering the broader base to make promotion up the pyramid possible. If the base does not expand rapidly enough, the whole career structure within the industry is challenged.

2.2 Critical success factors going forward

In an environment with changed and more exacting expectations from the client side, the ability to focus on client needs and deliver on them is a key advantage. Indeed, we would identify four critical success factors for strategy consulting firms in the future:

- **Clear positioning** – strategy consulting firms can achieve success by taking on large, full-scale operations, or by opting to focus on a specialist area with in-depth expertise.

- **Deep knowledge portfolio** – ideally to work across disciplines, e.g. with the ability to **combine** consulting on management and technology, function and industry, strategy and implementation. A further factor here is the growing importance of the public sector as key client, especially in Europe and Asia.

- **Internationalisation** – for the global servicing of clients, and global knowledge management. This implies a company organised on worldwide rather than local lines.

- **Supportive governance mechanisms** – enabling consulting firms to be adaptive and flexible, whilst remaining independent of institutional investors (e.g. equity firms), and with a strong value compass. Totally independent (e.g. Boston Consulting Group) vs. fully dependent consultancies (e.g. ex-PriceWaterhouseCoopers (IBM Consulting) form the two poles of a continuum of governance options.

How does Booz Allen Hamilton fit into this context? As a leading global strategy and technology consulting firm, the company is owned by 250 active officers worldwide. In terms of revenue, the company's annual turnover (US\$ 2.7 billion/year, with approximately 15,000 employees) places it in the upper echelon, and the company is organised on global lines under a "one firm" concept with a worldwide income sheet and profit and loss account.

With regard to the knowledge portfolio, at Booz Allen Hamilton the functions are grouped into the key areas of 'Organisation, Change, Leadership', 'IT' and 'Operations', whilst the industrial groupings cover aerospace, automotive, consumer products & life sciences, energy & utilities, financial services, healthcare, transportation, and telecommunications, media and technology. The company thus effectively combines functional and industry expertise, and capabilities in management and technology as well as in strategy and implementation. The company also has a strong presence in the area of public sector consulting, a growing market in Europe. Here it is able to leverage its in-depth expertise and experience in the US, where Booz Allen has a unique position in government consulting (e.g. over 3,000 consultants based in Washington DC).

In terms of internationalisation, the company generally deploys its staff worldwide to deliver maximum expertise to fit client needs, and assembles cross-disciplinary teams as the particular circumstances of the client demands. This clear focus on client needs enables Booz Allen to deliver solutions that yield real results (strategic breadth and functional depth). Evidence of this comes, amongst other studies, from the findings of the 2003 Kennedy data survey of 100 clients, evaluating 17 consulting firms, where Booz Allen Hamilton ranked number 1 for performance (expertise, quality, thought leadership) and for perception (client view of the company – see figures 2 and 3).

Market's Perception of Major Strategy Firms - 2003

Rating	Firm	% of Ratings That Were Favorable	% of Ratings That Were Unfavorable
3.78	**Booz Allen Hamilton**	65%	1%
3.73	Boston Consulting Group	63%	7%
3.64	McKinsey & Company	59%	12%
3.57	Mercer Management Consulting	47%	5%
3.55	Marakon Associates	36%	0%
3.54	A.T. Kearney	57%	9%
3.50	DiamondCluster	50%	6%
3.36	Bain & Company	42%	13%
3.33	Huron Consulting Group	25%	0%
3.32	Monitor Group	32%	5%
3.27	LEK Consulting	45%	18%

Fig. 2. Market's Perception of Major Strategy Firms (Source: Kennedy Information, 2003, p. 113)

**Client's Experience with
Major Consulting Firms - 2003**

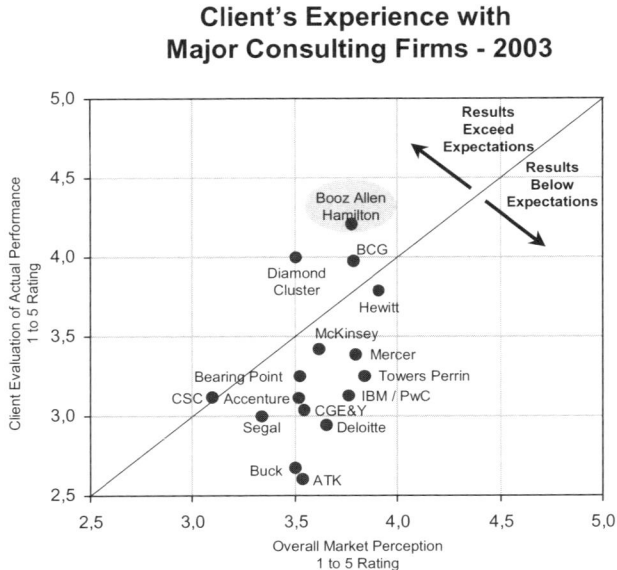

Fig. 3. Client's Experience with Major Consulting Firms (Source: Kennedy Information, 2003, p. 143)

Before we discuss the position at Booz Allen in respect of the final critical success factor outlined above, some reflection is called for on the basic principles of governance, as well as the importance of corporate values, in industry as a whole and in the consulting industry, in particular.

2.3 Governance, ownership, consulting and values

Currently there are various approaches to the issues of ownership, and the associated governance structures, within the consulting industry. Broadly speaking, these can be categorised into the following types:

- **Truly independent consultancies.** These are mostly organised in partnerships, with the partners owning the equity of the firm, financing and managing the company (e.g. Booz Allen Hamilton, Boston Consulting Group). Full, or "true", independence is ensured through debt-free governance, as at Booz Allen. This enables the company to act in a neutral, unbiased and completely independent way when providing consulting advice.

- **Consulting firms backed by a large IT company.** These companies often aim to leverage their IT link by combining what they offer (e.g. IT **services** with other consulting services), and by engaging in mutual cross-selling of strategic consulting and IT consulting (e.g. ex-PriceWaterhouseCoopers IBM Consulting). It is often the investors (i.e. the IT companies) who take the most important decisions and finance the company. Thus the consulting firm is heavily dependent on the investor, and the nature of the investor may "disqualify" the subsidiary from being able to provide consulting services to selected clients (e.g. the investor's competitors). Therefore, most consulting arms fight to gain maximum independence in their operations of this type.

- **Consulting firms backed by a major investor.** This model is similar to the previous one, and many of the same considerations apply. Examples of such consultancies are Bain, and to some extent DiamondCluster. The danger for these consultancies is that they may be reduced to being simply a conduit for venture capital investments.

- **Accounting firms with consulting arms.** A good example of this are KPMG and Bearing Point. These companies were forced to divest their consulting arms (e.g. Arthur Andersen and Andersen Consulting and "Accenture" have been broken up), but more recently the consulting side of operations is quietly being built up again. This trend will lead to spin-offs after an appropriate period (e.g. 5 to 10 years) to realise a profit – which would suggest an 'agenda' to grow the consulting arm with this in mind. Nevertheless, several regulators will take a close look at the possible conflicts of interests (e.g. in Germany, where a much stricter seperation of auditing and management consulting is envisioned by the government).

- **Publicly-owned companies**. Shares in these companies are traded on the stock market, but this makes them largely dependent on the vagaries of the stock market and thus sensitive to the associated pressures, such as the well-known shortcomings of quarterly reporting and profit expectations. The danger is that these companies will focus more on short-term impact than on natural, organic growth and long-term people development.

The advantages of the independent partnership over the other models outlined above is that partnerships are demonstrably independent, the advice which they offer is impartial (and not diverted into cross-selling approaches), and they are flexible and quick in their decision-making. All these qualities are essential in today's fast-pace business environment, with impartial advice being a major asset in becoming a trusted advisor to clients, especially during strategic transformation programmes. A potential disadvantage may arise from limitations with regard to larger investments. This in itself turned out to be an advantage during New Economy times where these firms showed greater conservatism over investments into the so-called dot-com companies.

Over the past few years we have witnessed some spectacular instances of the failure of corporate governance, notably in the company crashes and associated fraud scandals of 2001 and 2002 (Enron, Worldcom, Comroad). These have in turn given rise to a vigorous debate about corporate governance, with the evidence from these scandals indicating that they were brought about not simply by problems relating to corporate controlling and incentive systems, but also by issues relating to value concepts. In the light of this, the importance of a lived set of values cannot be overstated. In a climate where the confidence of others is increasingly a high-value business commodity, only a company secure in its own code of values can hope to engender third-party trust.

3. The value compass - its importance in business, and in a demanding economic climate

The code of values being espoused and lived within an organisation is the key to securing third-party trust, and the importance of value systems in business is an area which has been researched in detail by Booz Allen. In Spring 2003, Booz Allen carried out a survey of the 150 leading companies in the German-language region, on the issue of "Do values create value?" The companies were selected on the basis of reported turnover for 2001 and across all sectors. The figure below indicates how the focus of this Booz Allen initiative links in with the ongoing debate over corporate governance (figure 4).

Elements of the Corporate Governance Discussion

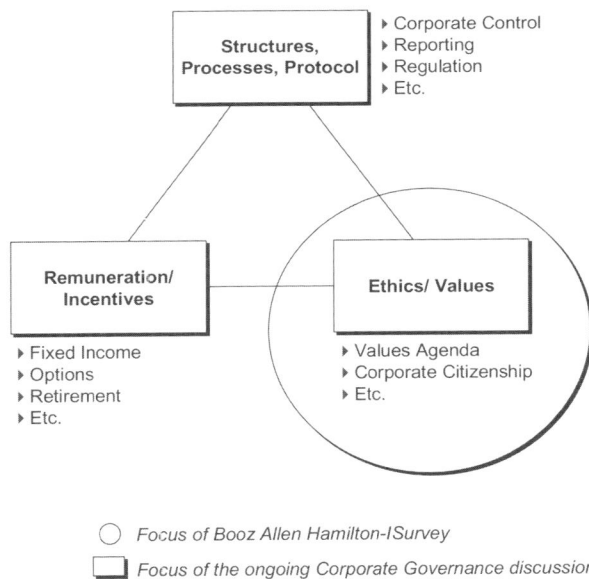

Fig. 4. Elements of Corporate Governance Discussion (Source: Burger et al., 2003, p. 4)

We are already seeing signs of a new awareness and renewed focus in the areas of salaries/incentives and structures/processes/regulations. Regulators, investors and the companies themselves are concentrating in particular on improved financial transparency, on expanding the reporting and liability obligations of the Management Boards, and on the salary structure for top management. The heightened exercise of corporate (self-)control is intended to send out the right management signals, in order to avoid any collapse in confidence in the probity and commercial wisdom of corporate management going forward.

The Booz Allen Hamilton survey found that over three-quarters of the Management Boards and top managers interviewed assume that values will gain in importance in future. In part, this is also a legacy of a period in which mergers, acquisitions and internationalisation have been the main drivers of corporate advancement that has led to companies with very different histories, guidelines and, in some instances, forms of conduct being brought together. Part of the challenge for the CEOs in these newly-formed company groups is to establish a new identity which all can share and which goes right to the heart of the values issue.

A further factor is the increasing cost pressures on companies, and thus the pressure for rationalisation processes. Carrying through such changes, whilst retaining the confidence of employees internally, is a key challenge, especially in a context where "knowledge as capital" is increasingly important. Under these conditions, losing the confidence of employees is like haemorrhaging capital, something no company can afford to do. If rationalisation is to be carried through successfully, then it is vital to ensure that there is no hint of arbitrariness or of knee-jerk reaction in the decisions taken.

3.1 Values – the economic benefit

What are the economic benefits of values? The Booz Allen survey found overwhelming agreement at senior management level that values generate economic benefits, and this belief is backed by several findings in the literature:

- **Kotter/Heskett (1992)**: companies with a strong culture driven by internal values have:
  - 4 times higher growth in turnover
  - 8 times higher growth in employment
  - a share price valued 12 times higher.

- **Collins/Porras (1994)**: visionary companies that live their values and place these above a pure profit mentality show growth over the long term 12 times stronger than that of the market.

- **Dearlove/Coomber (2002)**: employees in companies which live and implement their corporate values stay with the company for longer and are more motivated.

However, most of the companies surveyed did not make any quantitative measurement of the contribution to value which values made, which reflects the practical difficulties involved. Whilst a checklist approach can identify elements relating to corporate values which are (or are not) in place, it is far more problematic to quantify the effects which these elements have. Accordingly, the perceived benefits of values lies in their impact on the climate in which business is conducted, as evidenced in survey responses to the question, "What is the most important benefit of values for companies?" (figure 5).

What is the Most Important Benefit of Values for Companies?

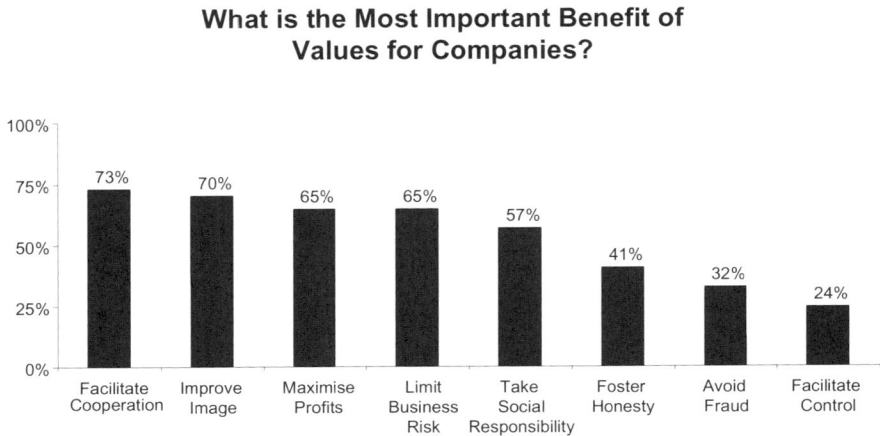

Fig. 5. What is the most important benefit of values for companies? (Source : Burger et al., 2003, p. 7)

People who share a common system of values and who identify positively with them are not only more motivated and more willing to perform – although this much at least has been demonstrated by the academic literature to date and is also generally acknowledged by companies. Above all, these employees share a common understanding of what is right and what is wrong. They submit to an informal control mechanism which contributes to the avoidance of inappropriate conduct, without an overarching structural or bureaucratic framework.

3.2 Which values?

The figure on the next page shows the range of responses to questions about the importance of particular values in their day-to-day business (figure 6).

It is noticeable that even the lowest score featured in this table is comfortably above the middle of the scale, and the average response (4,17) again reflects the fairly universal sense of the importance of values. Also noticeable is the relatively low position in the table of "shareholder value", which was the driving force behind much of the 1990s thinking on how to drive the values agenda forward. The events and scandals in 2001/2 have undermined confidence in the effectiveness of shareholder value in exerting influence over the "human failings" (such as the need to assert oneself, avarice, envy, fear, cronyism and a lack of openness). It was these failings which arguably come much closer to the heart of the problem than the structures which facilitated, concealed or removed from effective control the inappropriate conduct based on human failings. This is the point at which the debate about corporate governance and the arguments about a values agenda converge.

How Important are the Individual Values in Day-to-Day Business?

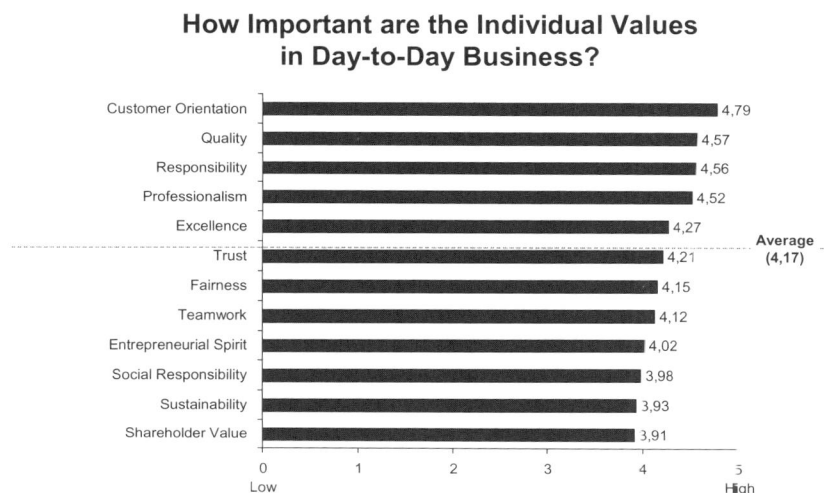

Fig. 6. How important are the individual values in day-to-day business? (Source : Burger et al., 2003, p. 9)

3.3 Shifting values

Values are undergoing change in much the same way as the organisational structures and the societies in which they are embedded. Value systems are thus not established to last for ever, but are geared to the changes in the company and in its environment. This holds true whether it is supported through a formal process in the company or not.

For some companies (although far from the majority), this change means subjecting their value systems to a process of fundamental commitment, examination or renewal, in some instances involving intensive employee participation and leadership training, for example in workshops, roadshows and seminars conducted around the world. This process reveals that there are values with varying degrees of importance within corporate value-systems, with "half-life values" existing alongside "core values", which are so closely bound up with the business system and the brand image that a change is not desirable or should only be undertaken with a great deal of caution and precision. Examples are, for instance, "reliability" or "safety" for an airline company, "punctuality" for a logistics company, "confidentiality" for companies in the private banking sector, or "honesty" for banking in general or for postal service companies. Companies that have recognised and acknowledged this "values DNA" as their own, place emphasis on the immense importance of such values, and ultimately on their durability. In doing so, it provides a common focus for the efforts of its employees and requires these efforts to be seen as a key priority and major driver of the long-term success of the company.

3.4 New values

Further changes to value systems are also being brought about through "imports" (mergers, acquisitions, preferred sources for recruiting, especially for managers), or through the understanding of values and the management style embraced by top management. The successful integration of values DNA and new impulses coming in from outside the company is a genuine challenge – also in terms of the importance of values for corporate governance. Many companies, it appears, have not yet been able to span a meaningful bridge across the chasm between comparatively traditional values and new, imported value-cultures. Here, the CEO in particular is perceived as having a prominent part to play.

3.5 Lived values

It is almost a commonplace in modern corporate thinking to consider the extent to which a company lives the set of values it embraces. In the public sector, too, a great deal of attention is paid to the seamlessness of the match between vision, policy and practice. The Booz Allen value survey indicated that, by comparison with the overwhelming majority (95%) which believed that values generate economic benefits, very few respondents (4%) felt that their company completely lived its set of values. For a significant group of those responding (36%), the perception is that values are only accorded a limited role in their company. It is worth reflecting on the effect which such a mismatch is likely to have on employee conduct, and on public perception of the company.

One specific area where this is likely to have an impact is business opportunities. Interestingly, the spread of responses to the Booz Allen value survey on this point is remarkably even across all categories (figure 7).

This compares with the responses to the question about the importance for the Management Board of balancing values against profit; here only 19% of responses ranked the importance in the bottom two categories, and only 3% considered it was "not at all" important for the Board.

**How Often Have You Passed
Up Business Opportunities for the
Sake of Safeguarding Values?**

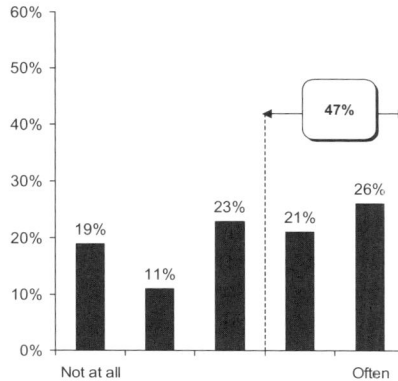

Fig. 7. How often have you passed up business opportunities for the sake of safeguarding values? (Source: Burger et al., 2003, p. 11)

3.6 Incentivising values

One possible mechanism to promote lived values within a company is to incorporate them into incentive schemes. This provides a degree of structure and standardisation across the company, and should contribute to "lived values". However, the Booz Allen survey indicated that this approach is not uniformly adopted – 55% of respondents indicating that their company did use incentives in this way, with 45% not using such incentives. Where some measurement of values was made, this was largely in terms of individual targets (figure 8).

The survey also revealed an even split when respondents were asked whether they would like to see more stringent instruments being applied to measure values within their companies. This may well reflect the ambivalence regarding the extent to which companies are viewed as promoting a set of values (see 2.5 above). If there is no perception within a company that values are important in practice, then there is little likelihood of 'grass roots' support for greater stringency in this area.

Measurement of Values

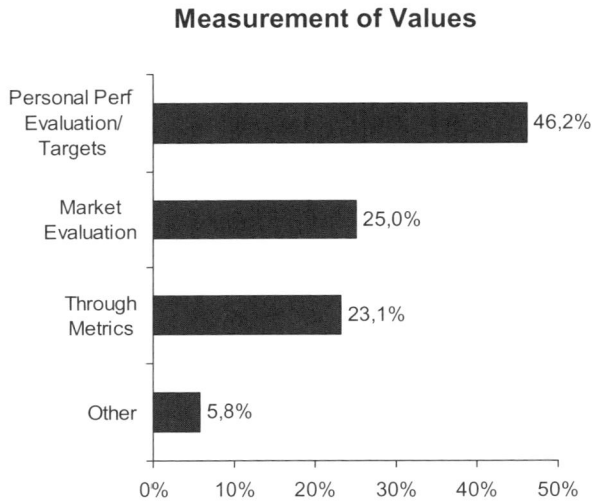

Fig. 8. Measurement of values (Source: Burger et al., 2003, p. 12)

3.7 Importance of CEO leadership

The survey responses indicate that the climate for a values agenda within a company is set to a considerable extent by the company management, at the highest levels. The Board Chairman, Management Board and Divisional Manager were cited as having the greatest influence in framing values within a company, and whilst it is possible to codify values into a set of rules and embed these in companies through the various appraisal mechanisms, at least at the qualitative level, such structural mechanisms are no guarantee that the values are being lived in a real sense (i.e. embraced and actively pursued by employees).

This same view was reflected in a question about the "anchoring mechanisms" to promote values being lived (figure 9).

What 'Anchoring Mechanism' Best Promotes Values Being 'Lived'?

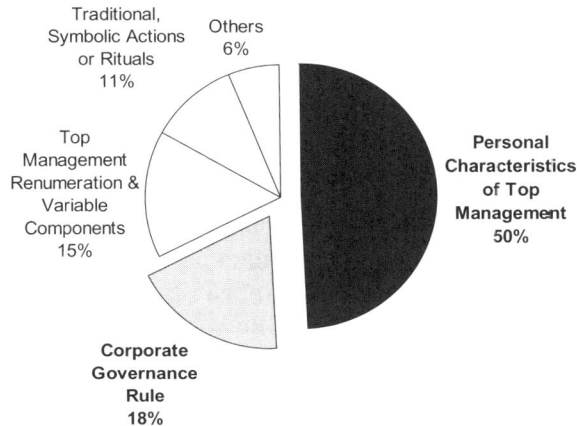

Traditional, Symbolic Actions or Rituals 11%

Others 6%

Top Management Renumeration & Variable Components 15%

Personal Characteristics of Top Management 50%

Corporate Governance Rule 18%

Fig. 9. What 'anchoring mechanism' best promotes values being 'lived'? (Source: Burger et al., 2003, p. 14)

There is a clear indication here that it is in the area of interpersonal interactions that the CEO and top management will be most effective in moving the values agenda forward. Structures, whilst important, are a codification and reinforcement for what is actually being "lived", i.e. experienced, through the promotion or sanctioning of value-relevant conduct within top management and through the career structure at that level.

4.   The importance of value systems for consulting firms

Given that this survey indicates the importance of values for the success of a company (albeit at the same time indicating a discrepancy between the status accorded to values and their importance 'on the ground' in many instances), and in view of the fact that it is the senior management levels which are perceived as being the key drivers of values within companies, what are the specific implications for strategy consulting companies?

On one level it is important that the consulting company itself is perceived as having a lived set of values. Where this 'value compass' is clearly embedded in a company's approach to consulting, it can assist in shaping fruitful relationships with clients. As with the issue of driving forward the values agenda within a company, it is again the interpersonal or "soft skills" aspect which is vital. In most instances, a consultant will achieve success not solely through his or her individual enthusiasm, commitment and expertise, but through building an intense client relationship. Such a relationship can only be based on mutual trust, and as such a major objective for the consultant is to become a "trusted advisor" to clients (see also 3.2 below).

A strong value compass is highly instrumental in achieving that objective. A clear sense of what defines absolute professionalism in terms of consulting, to be communicated through a strong codex of values (whether stated explicitly, or more likely, implicitly through evidence of that codex in its practical application), is a key element in creating a consistent perception of how the consulting service is delivered.

The appreciation and understanding of these aspects is something which is built up over time, but it is dependent on a long-standing and consistently lived set of values already being in place. Values cannot be "rolled out" on demand, but need to be internalised and given natural expression through the various challenges which present themselves. Values can thus be thought of as being part of the consultant's "brand equity", assisting in building the sense of trust right in a client relationship from the outset, and deepening that trust through shared experience.

4.1 The Booz Allen Hamilton governance model and value system

Booz Allen Hamilton is proud of its tradition as an independent consulting firm, and it enjoys a number of advantages as a consequence of this independence – greater flexibility, fast decision-making, the ability to act as a neutral, unbiased advisor at all times, and no conflicts with regard to competitiveness (e.g. the independent consulting firm is able to advise more than one player in the same segment).

As a result of its independent ownership structure and its global reach, the company has a strong and adaptable governance system. This allows the company to be adaptable and flexible in terms of decision-making, whilst independence from external influences (investors, banks etc.) is a further guarantee of full integrity for the client.

In tandem with effective governance systems, Booz Allen also places significant emphasis on values within the company. It has codified a core set of 10 professional values, and developing a deepened understanding and appreciation of these values are a part of the objectives of the company's in-post training. A consultant who is aware of what constitutes a professional approach will, for example, demonstrate a readiness to engage in explanation, to enable the client to appreciate why certain skills are being applied in a particular context. It is at this point that we are able to perceive the connection between the "professional value system" and the "lived values", which find their expression in the nature of the consultant-client relationship.

This aspect of lived values at Booz Allen Hamilton is also acknowledged by others – to give just two examples, Consulting Magazine ranks Booz Allen as number 1 on the areas of work-life balance, culture and morale, and "Working Mother" ranked Booz Allen among the top ten companies for working mothers.

Furthermore, these are values which impact on the way in which we relate to one another and which give expression to a certain "conduct". This is all the more important when one considers that the consulting firm is wholly-owned by the 220 partners. Being a "partner" at Booz Allen represents an obligation "to preserve" and "to prepare" the company for future generations of partners/employees.

The aspect which exemplifies these values is respect: respect for the individual and also for the individuality of each person with regard to religion, gender, nationality and their "lifestyle". As examples of this:

- "Unwillingness…" — ever to speak disparagingly of another member to anyone" describes the obligation to address differences of opinion factually and directly. It contains an expectation of professional conduct on the part of the consultant, and promotes a mature and open relationship style where disagreements can be aired appropriately and honestly.
- "Start with character, intelligence and industry…" was one of the first principles that Jim Allen, one of the founders, established. He placed character as the most important recruiting criterion before intelligence and industry expertise. For him, character was clearly the prerequisite to live corporate values and act as a role model. Character in this respect refers to the attitude and mindset towards colleagues, clients and – ultimately – towards society.

4.2   Lived values at Booz Allen Hamilton

The professional values mesh with a set of lived values and principles which have developed over time. We shall focus on three specific aspects – "tell it like it is", "do the right thing", and "commitment to community".

4.2.1 "Tell it like it is"

This is a counterbalance to the principle of supporting the client and not pursuing an 'own agenda' through consulting projects. The consultant is invariably engaged to tackle the thorny issues in management – the ones with no simple answers, and where the answers may not fit easily (or indeed at all) with the client agenda. In such instances, there is nothing to be gained by soft-pedalling – this can result in a damaging loss of credibility and trust in the consultant. The consultant has to be prepared to say unpopular things, and possibly handle the resultant short-term difficulties in the consultant-client relationship, in order to avoid what would otherwise be more serious damage to that relationship in the longer term. As with any relationship, overcoming difficulties is based on the mutual respect and credibility of the partners concerned – if this climate has been established, then the 'difficult things' can be spoken about more easily.

4.2.2 "Do the right thing"

This is an aspect which is bound up with issues of 'good governance'. There are recent examples of just how damaging the failure of managers or corporate governance and controlling mechanisms have been, both in material terms and in terms of business ideals. This aspect is even more vital for companies such as consulting firms, auditors, or legal advisors in maintaining their integrity in the marketplace. This integrity, together with the quality of their staff and their knowledge capital, are their most important assets. In practical terms, it involves things such as scrupulous respect for the confidentiality of data from or about the client, or establishing and maintaining "Chinese walls" between client teams when providing advice on internal organisation to companies competing in the same market. It also means having knowledge of external regulations and anchoring these in the internal corporate structures and in daily practice (e.g. with regard to insider trading or competition law).

Parallel to a framework where values are accorded importance and are put into practice on a day-to-day basis, measurement constantly takes place at Booz Allen Hamilton to ensure that the expectations based on these values are being fulfilled, and in instances of non-compliance sanctions are applied. This more formal approach ensures that values are institutionalised, i.e. they form part of any decision at Booz Allen, they govern how we work together and frame the parameters of our work. The values are also applied in partner/staff appraisals. Where there is clear evidence of non-compliance with values, this is viewed as threatening the Booz Allen culture and appropriate corrective action is taken (which in some circumstances may include termination of employment).

This sends out a clear message throughout the company about the importance of the culture of values – something which is, incidentally, wholly in line with the findings of the Booz Allen values survey, which indicated the clear need for leadership from the top down to fulfil a signal function in the discussion and creation of values. The survey also argued in favour of making values part of the day-to-day lived agenda, with corporate values flowing into clear rules of conduct for both internal and external dealings, and being measureable in the appraisal and incentive systems.

The successful linking of values and image is a success factor. At Booz Allen Hamilton, values are shared throughout the company – the partners and principals act as role models, and communicate values throughout the organisation (e.g. through mentoring). There is a general obligation for staff to pass these values on to future generations – as a company commitment states, "we hold the Firm in trust for generations to come and accept responsibility to pass on a strengthened heritage to our successors".

4.2.3 "Commitment to community"

This heading embraces the sense of responsibility towards future generations evident in the Booz Allen philosophy, placing the day-to-day business activity in a wider social context over time. However, it is equally possible to look at a consulting company – indeed, any company – from the viewpoint of how it "does the right thing" in terms of wider social responsibilities, by looking at the commitment it shows to going beyond the traditional client consultancy and assuming responsibility within the wider community.

Booz Allen´s community service efforts operate in a broader context of strategic philanthropy and corporate citizenship with a clearly expressed objective: "We work aggressively to earn and maintain our reputation as leading corporate citizens by giving back to the communities where we conduct business." (Booz Allen Hamilton, 2002, p. 44) For example, the company engages in community work on a voluntary basis or by taking on pro bono projects. Booz Allen people make their time and skills available to a wide variety of local community efforts across the globe. Examples of the company's involvement in this area include the 2002 Special Olympics where Booz Allen Hamilton supported the entire organisation of the event pro bono. Timothy Shriver, president and CEO of Special Olympics Inc. referred to the Booz Allen support as "… nothing short of monumental. The joy and development of the athletes and their achievements will be a reminder that the sometimes cold hard work of Booz Allen also has a power beyond the bottom line." Other examples include the Horizont project in Munich (an initiative to help women in need, where Booz Allen provided both financial assistance and expertise on specific projects for the charity), the Neediest Kids organization in Washington DC (a charitable organisation that raises funds for local school systems to help ensure that the most at-risk children have clothing and other items essential for their attendance and succeess at school, where Booz Allen provides office space and other infrastructure, public education material and the production of a new website as well as financial support) and the Prinzregententheater (another pro-bono project, to help restructure this Munich theatre and save it from closure), to name just a few.

The example of "commitment to community" demonstrates how a consulting company can be aware of obligations towards society, which go beyond the 'traditional client services', and live out this commitment both within and outside the firm. Furthermore, all three examples (4.2.1–4.2.3) illustrate how "values in the community" is not a one-way street – the company enjoys very real benefits in return for the commitment it shows in activeley assuming social responsibility both in its traditional consulting work and its wider areas of operations.

5. Summary

The above has underpinned the importance of values in the corporate context, and in particular in the context of consulting companies. It is apparent from the changes in corporate governance being demanded from many sides and already implemented in many companies, and in the wake of the corporate scandals at the start of this century, that we are set to see a period where one of the prime concerns for business is how to secure and maintain confidence – confidence both in the probity and soundness of internal controlling functions, and in the set of corporate values under which employees are operating.

One of the key elements in engendering such confidence is transparency. Where a company has a strong set of values and where these are clearly being lived in day-to-day business activity, will not go unnoticed by clients and will form a sound basis for developing the mutual trust, which is the bedrock of a commercial relationship that can be developed and deepened in the future.

Another key element in engendering confidence is a company's ability to demonstrate its independence of thought and philosophy. Where a company is bound by investor decisions or constrained in how it can operate, then clearly this restraint is likely to be perceived, calling into question the company's trustworthiness. The ability to forge independent partnerships is therefore of vital importance for consulting companies. It is essential for the client to know that its concerns are paramount, and for the consulting company "lived professionalism" and "lived values" are just as essential.

In consulting, in particular, lived professionalism and lived values begin for the individual with one key element, which Carl Hamilton, a co-founder of Booz Allen Hamilton described as "know your own blind spots." Consultants need to be aware of their own weaknesses and apply a "criterion of modesty" in their profession that will prevent them from "acting up". Otherwise they will fail.

References

Booz Allen Hamilton Annual Report (2002).

Burger, Christopher/Habbel, Rolf W./Gushurst, Klaus-Peter/Vogelsang, Gregor (2003): Werte schaffen Wert! Booz Allen Hamilton Publication, Munich.

Collins, James C./Porras, Jerry I. (1994): Built to Last: Successful Habits of Visionary Companies, HarperCollins, New York.

Czerniawska, Fiona/Lyons, L.. (2003): Competing in the European Consulting Market 2003-2004, Kennedy Information Inc., Peterborough, New Hampshire.

Dearlove, Des/Coomber, Stephen (2002): Corporate Values – How Organizational Values Can Drive Success, BrownHerron Publishing, Louisville, KY.

Kennedy Information (2003): The Client-Side Intelligence Report – Purchasing Behavior, Brand Awareness and Firm Perceptions, Peterborough.

Kotter, John P./Heskett, James L. (1992): Corporate Culture and Performance, Free Press, New York.

Parker, Andrew (2003): Management Consultants See Little Hope of Quick Recovery, in: Financial Times, 26.04.2003.

The Impact of Offshoring on the Consulting Industry

Fiona Czerniawska

1.   Introduction

Who would have thought, in the late 1990s, that the term offshoring would be on so many consultants' lips?

Five years ago the consulting industry was going through a period of unprecedented growth, fuelled by a combination of e-business opportunity and Y2K fear. No one batted an eye about regular increases to fee rates, such was the level of demand and scarcity of supply. A new generation of e-consulting firms had sprung from nothing to acquire revenues of hundreds of millions of dollars. Comparing the environment to the 19th century gold rush, everyone assumed that, even if the e-prospectors didn't strike it rich, the tool-sellers would.

Of course, the irony is that it was precisely these circumstances, which paved the way for offshoring. It was the shortage of skills in the run-up to the millennium that drove people to outsource IT work to India and the Far East. Having travelled to India in search of skills, western corporations have stayed to take advantage of lower labour rates at a time when domestic IT budgets are depressed. With budgetary pressure unabated, more functions have been deemed 'offshore-able'. Consultant after consultant will tell you that, for certain types of work, it has become impossible for them to win business without offering an offshoring component. "It's a given," said one.

But a greater irony may yet await us. While the collective revenues of offshoring suppliers still account for only a small percentage of the global consulting and IT services market, offshoring already has a bubble feel to it. Talk to offshoring suppliers and you hear the same language used by e-consulting firms at the height of the dot com revolution: "We're breaking the mould of professional services."

The slow-down in IT expenditure has affected the low-margin end of the market, too, and the first generation of suppliers face competition from even lower-cost producers such as China. With rivals snapping at their heels, Indian firms are looking to move up the value chain, using quality as a key differentiator in winning longer-term, more complex deals. But brand recognition, especially among the Western companies now considering offshore alternatives, remains poor. The last two years have seen offshore suppliers recruit sales and marketing staff in the Western economies where their clients are located, and forge alliances with onshore firms which have established access to key markets. Now, all the talk is of acquisition, giving these firms their own business consulting skills and experienced client relationship managers.

Moreover, like the e-consultancies before them, offshore service providers are already facing stiff retaliation from 'onshore' suppliers who have hired offshoring experts and/or sought alliances with offshore service providers to shore up profits in the face of increasing price pressure. Increasingly, onshore firms, too, are looking at acquisitions – of low-cost offshore facilities. Convergence between high-cost onshore and low-cost offshore firms is inevitable.

But which will be easier – onshore suppliers shedding their legacy of high-cost code cutters, or offshore suppliers building exclusive client relationships? Onshore suppliers' problems centre on people – current levels of onshore staff, how to recruit and develop people in the future – and the willingness of senior managers to drive through necessary changes. For offshore companies, the critical issue is how to increase their onshore presence without compromising their overall cost advantage.

Much has been written on the potential economic impact of offshoring on the organisations and economies that offshore. Very little research has been done on how offshoring may affect suppliers. This article will attempt to outline four quite different scenarios of the way in which offshoring may affect the consulting industry and analyse the types of firm likely to succeed or fail in each. It will, however, begin by examining the factors, which are likely to determine how suppliers will decide where to allocate their resources.

2. The uncertainties of demand

In forecasting future demand for offshoring, some of the assumptions suppliers are making may be more reliable than others. Clearly, no supplier is voluntarily going to give up access to valuable clients, especially when they are blue chip or where the services are high profile. A business without direct access to and an understanding of its end-customers is living on borrowed time. Forced to work through third parties, it runs the risk of being a back-office 'factory', supplying price sensitive services to its branded, customer-facing partners. Although most offshore suppliers entered Western markets via locally based consulting firms, they are now under pressure to own their client relationships. Building these relationships will require onshore, high-cost people, but how many?

There are, however, two areas where it is much harder to see how the future will play itself out:

1. Although almost everyone assumes that higher-end consulting services will continue to be carried out onshore, if not always onsite, clients' definition of onsite/offsite services has always been fickle. Where clients are accustomed to value added services being done offsite, they may also be comfortable offshoring more of these services than expected.

2. Many consulting firms believe that the opportunity to act as intermediaries in the offshoring market is substantial, helping clients negotiate the complexity of what is perceived to be a high-risk market. But there's a considerable difference between actual and perceived risk, as the technology bubble from 1998-2000 demonstrated.

2.1 How important is face-to-face contact?

Face-to-face contact is important to client-consultant and customer-supplier relationships because it increases effectiveness. Clients who are looking for effectiveness are more likely to want their consultants and IT service providers to work onsite with them and are less likely to countenance the work being done offsite, let alone offshore. Clients' desire for effectiveness, and consequently interaction, is therefore one of the main reasons why offshore companies believe they have to build their own onshore (onsite) resources if they are to move up the supplier pecking order. Similarly, onshore companies have derived comfort from what they see as a clear line over which offshoring cannot cross.

But clients do not just want effectiveness: they are also looking for efficiency and economy (the 'Three Es'). In a perfect world, clients want all three pieces of this cake. In practice, however, one of these goals is more important than the others. And it is up to the client to prioritise the goals. For example, a client under budgetary pressure may choose to sacrifice, say, five percent of effectiveness for a 50 percent reduction in costs. A client with a tight deadline to make is going to be most worried about efficiency.

The point at which face-to-face contact ceases to be essential and starts to be merely a nice-to-have is therefore a fluid one. Over the last two years, recessionary conditions have made efficiency and economy more important than effectiveness. While this continues to be the case, the proportion of a consulting or IT services project that requires face-to-face interaction will shrink. Once a recovery comes, this trend may be reversed: We only have to think back to the internet mania of the late 1990s to see how comparatively unimportant cost (economy) can be.

In shifting the balance from effectiveness to efficiency, and from efficiency to economy, two factors predominate: the availability of alternative ways of working and the extent to which clients feel there is scope for cutting costs. These two factors also tell us how important (or not) face-to-face interaction is likely to be in the client-consultant, customer-supplier relationships of the future, and therefore the balance of onshore/offshore resources a supplier will need.

People working side-by-side are better able to exchange information, they can plumb each other's experience and challenge their assumptions, and they are more capable of handling complexity and being flexible. With interaction, there is more trust and less bureaucracy. Or so we think. Ten years ago, at the height of the business process re-engineering frenzy, the focus was on breaking down internal barriers in order to see processes end-to-end. Today, the opposite is true: efficiency comes from breaking processes down into their component parts. But, while it is hard to believe that every process can be offshored in its entirety, the more organizations break down their components, so that each stage of it can be done by highly-specialized, comparatively independent teams, the more likely it is that some of a process can be offshored. You end up with specialized teams spread across the world. Internal centres of excellence will be mirrored by external suppliers, each of which plays a precise role in what becomes a much more complex picture.

Chief information officers have only one thing on their minds these days: getting more for less. While breaking a process down into its component parts is seen to create greater scope for efficiency, clients will only move into economy mode while they believe there is scope to cut costs. Indeed, interaction is inversely proportionate to cost pressure. A client who is wholly focused on negotiating the lowest possible price is not going to set much store by something as intangible and apparently ephemeral as interaction. They want the job done – and they want it done cheaply. Interaction may be important if a consultant or service provider is to do their job effectively, but it is icing on the cake when they have to do it economically.

Indeed, the wage differentials look even more attractive when placed against the scarcity of qualified labour in many Western economies. US economic growth in the 1990s, which resulted in a lack of available domestic labour, was a major boost to the offshore industry. Even today, after two years of lacklustre economic performance, which finds more than 200,000 computer and math professionals unemployed, it is still estimated that there will be a shortfall of more than 10 million workers in the US by 2010 (US Bureau of Labor Statistics, April 2003). Of course, such predictions rely heavily on growth in GDP: the truth is that nobody knows how big the actual shortfall will be. However, offshore suppliers are likely to benefit: from the increasing use of contractors in IT departments (the Meta Group predicts that 50% of IT employees could shift to contract work by 2007, analogous with the shift in manufacturing jobs 30 years ago); from increasing specialization, which in turn is driving IT managers to look for a flexible mix of skills; and from the growing preference to buy rather than build IT applications (which requires fewer in-house programmers).

Barring major political and social upheaval, it is hard to see the supply of qualified labour in countries such as India and China drying up in the foreseeable future. The sustainability of the wage differential is, however, more questionable. While conventional outsourcing allowed organizations to cut costs in two ways (by reducing both the number of people required for a particular activity and the average cost per person), offshoring – because it has been seen as the next logical step after outsourcing – has delivered savings purely in terms of the average cost per person.

Power will always lie with the buyers. There will always be another, even lower cost source of labour emerging, even if these become sub-contractors to today's offshorers. Thus, a US firm will have a relationship with an Indian one, which will have a relationship with a Vietnamese one – and so on. What matters is being able to figure out the cascade effect.

2.2   How risky will offshoring be perceived to be?

As with any other business decision, offshoring involves risk – the risk that the new service may not meet expectations; that it will turn out to be more expensive than planned; that political upheaval in the country where the offshore supplier is based will undermine confidence. As these risks become better understood and more accurately quantified, the need to make special efforts to manage them – in this instance, the use of intermediaries to manage offshoring contracts – declines.

It is the speed of that decline that is the critical uncertainty here. If the perceived level of risk remains high, then those intermediaries can look forward to a relatively comfortable, sustainable business. But if clients decide they can manage their own risks, then the future of the intermediary looks shaky.

So are we in danger of creating a bubble here in which clients, swept up by the offshoring equivalent of internet fever, believe that the risks involved are now negligible? Opinion is divided. "As with the dot.com era, it all comes down to the business case," said one consultant I spoke to. "There'll always be people who jump on the bandwagon without due process. It's amazing how some corporations are prepared to gamble with their reputations." But another disagrees: "Yes, there's overselling. There'll always be clients who have a go and get it wrong, who take an optimistic view of what is a complicated issue. But it's not analogous to the e-bubble: companies have been outsourcing for the last 30 years. They're more aware of the issues and there's more scrutiny of their decisions."

Recent history suggests that intermediaries have a poor life expectancy, sustained only where information is scarce, procurement processes inefficient and value-add unclear. Intermediaries are primarily a function of an immature market: they bring a degree of comfort to companies that do not know India or the Far East. But how many of the multinational corporations considering offshoring are in this position today, let alone in five years time?

3.   Four scenarios for the future of offshoring

These two variables – the acceptable level of interaction between client and service provider and clients' perceived level of risk with offshoring activities – can be used as the basis for four scenarios of the future impact of offshoring.

Four Scenarios for the Future Impact of Offshoring

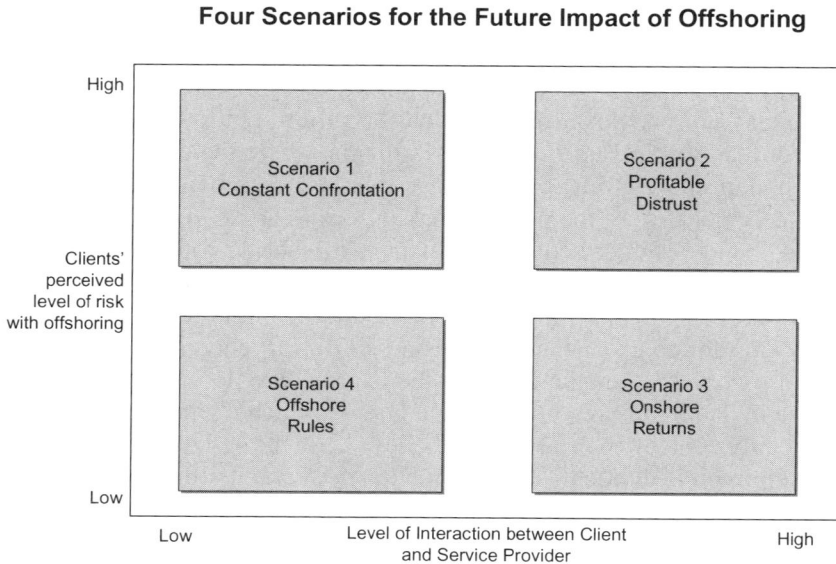

Fig. 1. Four scenarios for the future impact of offshoring

3.1 Scenario 1: Constant confrontation (High Risk – Low Interaction)

Long-term stagnation of the global economy will mean that corporations have not progressed beyond the cost-cutting agenda of the millennium's start. Managers brought up to value cost control over innovation will always look for new ways to pare their operations rather than build revenue. The market for outsourcing will grow at the expense of consulting services, much as it did from 2001 to 2003. However, attempts by offshore companies to move up the value chain will fall flat and most firms will be confined to competing on price. Breaking out of this cycle in order to invest in innovative, potentially higher margin services will prove impossible.

While the market for offshoring has grown significantly and now extends to medium as well as large scale organizations, trust between the service providers and clients has not. Reinforced by constant haggling over price, client-supplier relationships are at an all time low. The average length of an outsourcing project has fallen, and it is not uncommon for clients to terminate contracts before they expire to switch to another, even lower-cost supplier. Unwilling to pay the premium fees demanded by the intermediary firms, clients have established their own procurement departments, staffed by outsourcing and offshoring experts who cultivate a confrontational style.

Larger offshore suppliers have responded in kind, recruiting (or acquiring) their own class of aggressive, onshore account managers. These high-cost resources have cut further into their margins, leaving them with little room to invest in training and development of their own offshore people. A vicious circle has ensued in which service quality and flexibility has been sacrificed in favour of price.

Smaller offshore suppliers, unable to invest even in account managers, survive only as 'factory' partners for onshore suppliers. There is constant churn, as offshore players enter and exit the market.

Onshore firms with significant offshore facilities have fared better, able to exploit their reputations and existing client relationships in order to negotiate better deals than their offshore competitors. Protecting their market share has cost them dearly in margin terms, as the process of migrating more services overseas (often through acquisition of smaller offshore suppliers) has taken longer than anticipated. Onshore firms without substantial offshore resources have seen their revenues shrink significantly.

3.2 Scenario 2: Profitable distrust (High Risk – High Interaction)

Continuing concerns over the political and social stability of low-cost economies means that offshoring will be seen as a high-risk strategy. Stories abound of abandoned projects and unmet expectations. As a result, the market for offshoring across medium-sized enterprises will fail to materialize. Larger companies, still attracted by the cost differentials, manage the risk by relying heavily on the advice of independent intermediaries. However, the role of these agents will change: Rather than provide advice on how to negotiate deals, the intermediaries will be used to manage the offshore supplier. Complex sub-contracting arrangements will ensure that intermediaries' liabilities are covered – at least on paper.

The failure of the middle market to open up has driven many smaller suppliers out of business and deterred potential entrants, leaving a supply-side that has consolidated around a small number of large-scale offshore companies.

Attempts by these firms to establish onshore operations have foundered on endemic client distrust. The doubts have grown to the point that offshore business development efforts are now wholly focused on the intermediary market. Even here, it is proving impossible to build relationships and counterproductive to forge alliances: in order to preserve their independence, intermediaries issue highly structured requests for proposals and the space for personal relationships is minimal. Legal fees soar .

With so high an upfront investment, the average offshore contract duration is rising. Intermediary firms mitigate their own risk by tending to work with a small group of well-known and reputable suppliers, making it almost impossible for new suppliers to enter the market.

The importance of independence also means that those onshore suppliers that combined offering advice and brokering deals with their own offshore facilities have had to choose between the two. Some have chosen to become intermediaries: while their revenues have fallen, profit margins have remained high. Other firms have gone down the offshore route and have cut their onshore resources back severely. These firms now compete directly with other offshore firms, but their brands and reputations give them an edge. This is fortuitous, as it is not a strategy they could easily reverse: pigeon-holed by intermediaries and with comparatively little direct client contact, suppliers are hard-pressed to develop the innovative agenda that would allow them to establish closer client relationships.

3.3 Scenario 3: Onshore returns (Low Risk – High Interaction)

A gradual upturn in the world economy post-2003 will put a break on the seemingly inexorable expansion of offshoring. Clients will turn increasingly to their more familiar, onshore suppliers to explore revenue-generating ideas: demand for outsourcing and offshoring has plateaued, while demand for traditional management consulting will grow.

This sea change has allowed onshore firms to reassert their dominance in the market place, and created a virtuous circle in which clients are willing to collaborate in developing performance improvement ideas. Offshore companies have not been able to build their brands before consulting re-establishes itself. So offshore has failed to move up the value chain. Lower-than-expected growth in offshoring revenues and increasingly insurmountable difficulties in penetrating markets have forced these companies to abandon their plans for onshore recruitment and acquisition. The offshore firms have been forced to continue partnering with onshore suppliers. With offshoring seen as a self-contained option, there's little pressure from clients to go beyond these partnering arrangements.

Suppliers are polarized between client facing, big-branded firms and back-office "factories". Lacking any impetuous to consolidate around brands, the offshore industry has fragmented as it struggles to cope with the increasingly specialized demands of a maturing client base. Specialization means that the value of offshoring contracts is smaller; however, the fact that offshoring is seen as a given means they also cover a long period.

The renaissance of onshore firms and an increasingly well-understood market have decimated the once-burgeoning market for intermediaries. Most firms in this sphere have either been subsumed into the larger onshore firms or simply disappeared.

3.4 Scenario 4: Offshore Rules (Low Risk – Low Interaction)

A succession of stories in the press, highlighting the proven advantages of offshoring, together with continuing budgetary pressure on clients, will result in an explosion of the offshoring market. Clients, concerned about the capacity of the offshore industry, will agree to long-term, fixed price contracts – even with relatively unknown offshore suppliers – as a hedge against future increases in labour costs.

Offshore suppliers have grown rapidly. Increased access to clients has meant that many of the larger firms have succeeded in their aspirations to move up the value chain. Mounting revenues have allowed them to expand their onshore resource base without compromising their economic advantage. Some have acquired onshore suppliers to boost their immediate presence in local markets. Most have abandoned any pretence of working through third-party, onshore partners.

Faced with this onslaught, high-cost onshore suppliers have performed badly. Unable to grow their nascent offshore facilities in line with demand, traditional consulting firms have lost ground to their offshore rivals. Moreover, as the definition of what is regarded as offshore-able has expanded, these firms have found their traditional markets shrinking as well. Indeed, onshore firms are inadvertently aiding this process. By offshoring back-office functions in an effort to shore up margins and cutting fee rates, they have been cannibalising their own cost base.

Attempts to develop innovative new services have largely fallen on deaf ears, leaving these suppliers struggling to articulate their raison d'être. Some onshore firms have succeeded in developing innovative services which allow them to sidestep encroaching commoditisation, but many more, unable to innovate effectively, have shrunk to the point where they become targets for potential acquisition.

The rapid maturation and acceptability of offshoring has reduced the role intermediaries to a minimum. Clients shortlist potential offshore suppliers on the basis of their brand and reputation. Only in specialized fields, where the sheer number of potential suppliers becomes a problem, do intermediaries have any recognized value to add.

4. Winners and losers

As it is not yet clear which of these scenarios will be the closest to reality, arguing that one particular firm will do better than another would be premature. What we can say is that some types of firms are better positioned to cope with the vagaries of different scenarios than others. The 'winning' firms are those with what could be term strategic resilience: they are likely to perform well under all potential scenarios; 'losing' firms may do well in one or two situations, but will fare extremely badly in others.

4.1 Scenario 1: Constant confrontation

Succeeding in this scenario will require significant resources both onshore and offshore. Suppliers will need locally based account managers and offshoring experts if they are to negotiate effectively with clients' own, in-house procurement teams, but will only be able to secure contracts if they have sufficient offshore resources to keep the overall costs low. Size will be an advantage here: with price competition intense, being able to achieve economies of scale will be an important source of competitive advantage. The winners in this scenario therefore fall into two main categories: Large-scale onshore firms with a sizeable offshore presence which they are in the process of growing rapidly; and large-scale offshore firms already building onshore account managers and consulting teams. Intermediaries, in general, fare badly in this scenario, squeezed out by a combination of direct negotiation between clients and suppliers with offshore facilities, and fierce price competition.

4.2 Scenario 2: Profitable distrust

In contrast the previous scenario, it is the intermediary firms which are likely to perform best in this environment, where clients choose to cushion themselves against the perceived risks by using third-party advisors, negotiators, even deal-makers. Among this segment of the industry, those prepared to take a hands-on role fare better than those staking out the purely advisory role. Also likely to benefit from this scenario are the larger, better branded offshore companies. Combining low costs with the security of comparatively well-known names, these firms will appear to be particularly attractive partners from the point of view of the intermediaries that will be responsible for brokering the majority of offshoring deals. The suppliers likely to suffer most in this scenario are those who are likely to be pursuing dual strategies – positioning themselves as sourcing advisers on the one hand, while also providing offshoring services on the other. These firms may suffer on several fronts. They may find it hard to compete on price, as they will have a higher proportion of onshore resources to finance than their offshore rivals. Their downstream delivery resources will also make it hard for them to be credibly independent.

4.3 Scenario 3: Onshore returns

Unquestionably, the primary beneficiaries under this scenario will be the conventional, onshore management consulting firms. As clients' attention swings back to consider revenue generating ideas, instead of the cost-cutting strategies they have pursued since 2001, they are more likely to turn to the onshore players they have historically used in this capacity. Onshore IT services and consulting firms will also do well, as clients look to buyer higher-end IT skills, rather than commodity body shopping. Scenario 3 is not necessarily hostile to offshore suppliers. Providing they have had the opportunity both to develop and to be seen to have developed more innovative, added value services, they may offer some clients an attractive alternative to their traditional suppliers. This advantage is, however, likely to be confined to the largest offshore suppliers which have the resources and funding to diversify. Even here, the key question will be time. If economic recovery is swift, then even the largest offshore supplier may find the window of opportunity has been too small. The chief casualties are the pure intermediaries whose existence is predicated on a high-risk, complex offshoring market, and the offshore providers that, either because of their smaller size or less well-known brand, find it harder to compete with the resurgence of the onshore industry.

4.4 Scenario 4: Offshore rules

Access to offshore resources will be a critical determinant of success in this scenario. Not surprisingly, therefore, it is offshore firms which stand to do best out of it, and may even find themselves turning clients away, much as the fastest growing e-business consulting firms did in 1998-2000. Outside this segment, performance is likely to be patchy. While most onshore suppliers are likely to perform badly in this scenario, those that are rapidly growing offshore facilities may fare better. Offset against this will be the extent to which some of their traditionally onshore services are migrating offshore, as clients look to jump on a rapidly forming bandwagon. Similarly, while most intermediaries have been marginalized by clients' preference for dealing with offshore suppliers directly, a minority may perform comparatively well because of their specialist expertise.

Overview of Service Providers' Risk/Reward Profiles

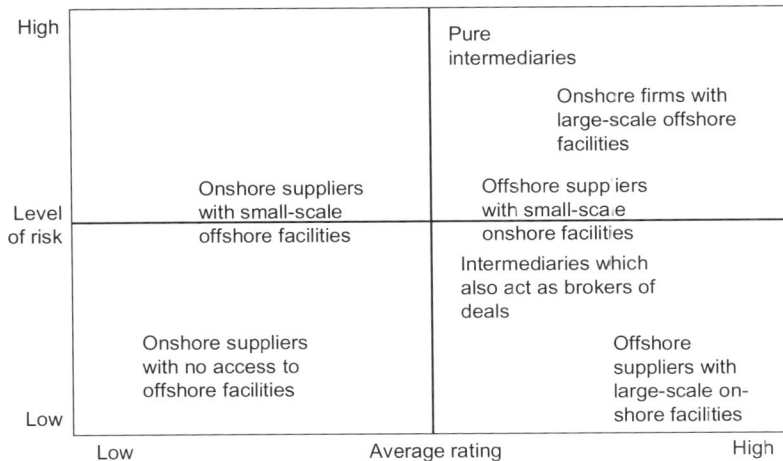

Fig. 2. Overview of service providers' risk/reward profiles

Figure 2 compares the likely fate overall of different types of supplier in terms of
1. their average rating across all four scenarios
2. the extent to which their rating varies from scenario to scenario, with a high level of variance indicates a high level of risk, and a low level of variance indicates a low level of risk.

Offshore firms which are already building their own onshore facilities and intermediary firms which also help to broker deals combine the lowest level of risk with the highest average rating across all four scenarios and are therefore likely to be the most successful at withstanding the potential threats of offshoring and/or exploiting its possible opportunities.

Looking at firms' relative positions overall, it appears that the consulting, outsourcing and IT services industries stand to gain, rather than lose, from offshoring (there are more firms on the right hand side of the matrix in Figure 2 than on the left). However, it is also a high-risk future in which long-term survival cannot be guaranteed. For many firms, however, success lies on a knife edge.

About the Authors

FIONA CZERNIAWSKA, PhD is the Director of the UK Management Consultancies Association's Think Tank, and Founder and Managing Director of Arkimeda, a firm that specialises in researching and consulting on strategic issues in the consulting industry. Fiona Czerniawska has more than 15 years experience as a management consultant, primarily working in the areas of marketing and strategy, and now speaks and writes extensively on the consulting industry and related issues. Her books include: *Management Consultancy: What Next?* (2001) and *Value-Based Consulting* (2002). She is also the author of a variety of commercial reports on the consulting industry, including *The European Consulting Market* (2002) and *Offshore Consulting: Benchmarking Future Success* (2003) Her most recent book is *The Intelligent Client* (2002). Fiona Czerniawska graduated from Oxford and has a PhD from the University of London.

JONATHAN DAY is the Managing Director, Europe, of the Monitor Group's Human Assets practice. Monitor is an international firm with a range of advisory and merchant banking services, all aimed at helping clients become more competitive. Monitor's Human Assets practice helps clients on matters of leadership and organisational development.
At the time this chapter was written, Jonathan Day was a Partner in the London office of McKinsey & Company, which he joined in 1990. His focus in McKinsey was on organisation, leadership and corporate strategy for global industrial firms. His undergraduate degree is from the Johns Hopkins University, with graduate studies at Johns Hopkins, Stanford University and the University of Chicago. Before joining McKinsey, Jonathan Day was the founder of The Amethyst Corporation, a Chicago-based consulting firm, and an Adjunct Professor at Carnegie-Mellon University, Pittsburgh.

Dr. JOACHIM DEINLEIN is a Project Manager at Booz Allen Hamilton, based in the Munich office. He received his degree in 1997 from the Otto-Friedrich-University in Bamberg and his doctorate from the EUROPEAN BUSINESS SCHOOL, Schloss Reichartshausen in 2003. He joined Booz Allen Hamilton in April 1998. After two years of broad exposure to diverse industries, Joachim Deinlein has specialised since 2000 in strategy and operations work in the automotive sector. His dominant focus is on sales and marketing topics such as retail network development, asset lifetime value, campaign effectiveness, aftersales, telematics, and back office efficiency.

Dr. KLAUS-PETER GUSHURST is a Partner with Booz Allen Hamilton, based in the Munich office. He is the Managing Director for Germany, Switzerland and Austria, and a member of the Global Board of Directors of Booz Allen Hamilton. He studied economics, business and political science at the Albert-Ludwigs-University in Freiburg where he received his degree in economics in 1988 and completed his doctorate in business studies in 1990, both with honours. Klaus-Peter Gushurst joined Booz Allen Hamilton in 1990, and in his more than 15 years in consulting has worked in several industries gaining a wealth of experience in strategy and operations work. Klaus-Peter Gushurst has led several assignments for key clients in Europe, the US and Japan. His main interests are in the financial services and the automotive industry with a functional focus on strategy-based transformation programmes and corporate governance, the role of the board of management, CEO/CFO issues, and the organisational set-up of multinational industries. Klaus-Peter Gushurst lives with his family south of Munich.

Dr. DIETER HEUSKEL is a Senior Vice President in the Düsseldorf office of The Boston Consulting Group, a member of BCG's worldwide Executive Committee, and Chair of BCG's Management Team for Germany, Austria, and Greece. He joined BCG in 1980 and is co-founder of the Düsseldorf office. His main areas of expertise include strategy development and portfolio management for diversified companies and change projects. In his many interviews and articles he presents innovative and often controversial concepts on topics such as 'premium conglomerates', business migration, and deconstruction. He is the author of the book *Wettbewerb jenseits von Industriegrenzen. Aufbruch zu neuen Wachstumsstrategien* (1999). He has been a member of the Board of Editors for the *Zeitschrift für Betriebswirtschaftslehre* since 1999, and in the same year he initiated BCG's Europe-wide pro bono project business@school. Dieter Heuskel lives with his family near Düsseldorf.

DAVID H. MAISTER is a Consultant specialising in advising professional service firms worldwide. For more than two decades he has advised these firms on the full range of managerial and strategic issues. He is the author of five best-selling books about professional firms, including *Managing the Professional Service Firm* (1993) and *First Among Equals* (2002). Prior to launching his consulting practice, he was a Professor at the Harvard Business School. A native of Great Britain, David Maister was educated at the University of Birmingham, the London School of Economics and the Harvard Business School. He lives with his wife in Boston, Massachusetts.

ANSGAR RICHTER, PhD is an Assistant Professor in the Department of International Management & Consulting at the EUROPEAN BUSINESS SCHOOL (ebs), Schloss Reichartshausen near Frankfurt, Germany. Before joining the ebs in summer 2002, he worked as a management consultant with McKinsey & Company, Inc. He studied philosophy and economics in Frankfurt and Bochum before joining the London School of Economics where he completed an M.Sc. in Industrial Relations and Personnel Management and a PhD in Management. He also spent some time as a visiting scholar at the University of California at Berkeley. Ansgar Richter's special areas of interest include strategic organisation and the internal structure of consulting firms, and he has published extensively on these and other topics. He is married and lives with his wife and two children in Frankfurt.

FRANK RIEMENSPERGER is the Managing Partner of Accenture's 'Products' Business Unit in Germany, Switzerland and Austria. Furthermore, he is the Deputy Country Managing Director of Accenture Germany. In this function, he is responsible for, among others, devising business strategy and coordinating new business opportunities across industries. During his career Frank Riemensperger has specialised in defining and delivering large-scale business transformation programmes. He studied in Germany and the United States and holds a degree in business information systems. He is married and lives with his wife and three children in the Rhein-Main Area.

Dr. BURKHARD SCHWENKER is Spokesman of the Executive Committee of Roland Berger Strategy Consultants. He studied mathematics and business administration at the University of Bielefeld from 1977 to 1981. He launched his professional career at PWA Papierwerke Waldhof-Aschaffenburg AG, where he last worked as a board assistant. He was awarded a doctoral degree by the University of Flensburg for his dissertation on competition in service companies in 1989. In the same year, he joined the Corporate Strategy and Organization Competence Center of Roland Berger Strategy Consultants and started to build up the Hamburg office. He was elected Partner in 1992 and appointed Head of the Competence Center in 1994. Burkhard Schwenker was a key figure in the management buyout negotiations with Deutsche Bank in 1998, the year in which the Partners elected him to the Executive Committee. In this capacity, he was in charge of corporate development, financial planning and analysis, product development and knowledge management. In July 2003 Burkhard Schwenker became Spokesman of the Executive Committee of Roland Berger Strategy Consultants, taking over from the company's founder, Roland Berger. He is married, has three children and lives in Hamburg.

Dr. FRANZ-JOSEF SEIDENSTICKER is the Managing Director of Bain & Company Germany, Inc. He has worked extensively in a wide range of industries throughout Europe, including engineering, high-tech, telecommunication and process industry. Franz-Josef Seidensticker specialises in strategy and corporate development, logistics and distribution, organisation and re-engineering. He earned a degree in business administration from the University of Paderborn, an MBA from the Worcester Polytechnic Institute in the USA, and his doctoral degree from the University of St. Gallen.

Prof. Dr. TOM SOMMERLATTE is Chairman of Arthur D. Little GmbH. He has over thirty years of international consulting experience, mainly in the areas of strategy and innovation consulting for large global corporations in industries with substantial R&D content. As the Managing Director of Arthur D. Little Europe, he led the development of the firm in Germany, Austria, Switzerland, France, the UK, Scandinavia, the Benelux, Italy, Spain/Portugal, and Eastern Europe. He has also been a spearhead of Arthur D. Little's global Technology and Innovation Management Consulting Practice. He studied physical chemistry and chemical engineering at the Universities of Berlin, Rochester/N.Y. and Paris and obtained his doctoral degree at the latter. He also obtained an MBA at the European Institute of Business Administration, INSEAD. He is the author of over 15 books on management issues. He served as President of the German Association of Management Consultants of which he is now an honorary member. He holds a Professorship at the University of Kassel where he lectures on Systems Research and Design. Tom Sommerlatte is married and has eleven children.

Prof. Dr. JEAN-PAUL THOMMEN is Professor of Business Administration, in particular Organisational Behaviour and Human Resource Management at the EUROPEAN BUSINESS SCHOOL, Schloss Reichartshausen, Germany. He also holds an Adjunct Professorship at the University of Zurich and is Visiting Lecturer at the University of St. Gallen. Professor Thommen is a member of numerous academic associations and committees, and serves on several boards. His main areas of research are general business administration, business ethics, change management, organisational learning and coaching. He has published extensively in these and other areas. Professor Thommen is married and lives with his wife in Zürich.

MICHAEL TRÄM is Chairman of the Management Board of the globally operating management consultancy A.T. Kearney. He studied economics and law in Saarbrücken and New York. Before joining A.T. Kearney in 1989, he worked for the lawyer's office Coudert Brothers in the United States and for Banque Populaire in France. As a consultant Michael Träm works with the worldwide leading enterprises, e.g. in banking, telecommunications and high tech, and in the automotive industry. His main consulting focus is on the preparation and implementation of mergers and acquisitions, a subject on which he has published several books and articles.

DR. WOLFGANG ZILLESSEN is Managing Partner with Deloitte, based in Frankfurt. He leads the German Manufacturing Practice and is a member of the European Consulting Leadership Team. Wolfgang Zillessen has 15 years of professional experience in management consulting. His focus is on corporate strategy, restructuring and reorganisation, as well as on mergers and acquisitions and transaction support for private equity firms and corporates. Before joining Deloitte, Wolfgang Zillessen worked for four years for the Dutch electronics group Philips and spent 12 years with Arthur D. Little, prior to his departure as Managing Director for their German operations. He studied economics at the RWTH Aachen and the University of Cologne and obtained a doctoral degree in business administration and computer science.

Index of Names